BACKROADS

of

SOUTH CAROLINA

BACKROADS

— of —

SOUTH CAROLINA

*Your Guide to South Carolina's Most
Scenic Backroad Adventures*

TEXT AND PHOTOGRAPHY BY

PAUL M. FRANKLIN AND

NANCY MIKULA

Voyageur Press

DEDICATION

To my father, Jim Franklin: test pilot, inventor, and friend, who instilled in me a passion for adventure and, when I was ready, set me free at the edge of the great American highway and told me to write when I could.

— Paul M. Franklin

To my mom, Evelyn Mikula, for sharing her love of exploring country roads and byways and encouraging me to discover what lies around the next bend.

— Nancy Mikula

First published in 2006 by Voyageur Press, an imprint of MBI Publishing Company, Galtier Plaza, Suite 200, 380 Jackson Street, St. Paul, MN 55101-3885 USA

Voyageur Press titles are also available at discounts in bulk quantity for industrial or sales-promotional use. For details write to Special Sales Manager at MBI Publishing Company, Galtier Plaza, Suite 200, 380 Jackson Street, St. Paul, MN 55101-3885 USA.

Franklin, Paul M.
Backroads of South Carolina : your guide to South Carolina's most scenic backroad adventures / by Paul M. Franklin and Nancy Mikula.
    p. cm.
 ISBN-13: 978-0-7603-2640-4 (softbound)
 ISBN-10: 0-7603-2640-1 (softbound)
 1. South Carolina—Tours. 2. Scenic byways—South Carolina—Guidebooks. 3. Automobile travel—South Carolina—Guidebooks. 4. South Carolina—Pictorial works. I. Mikula, Nancy, 1947- II. Title.
F267.3.F73 2006
917.5704'44—dc22

        2006024851

Editor: Leah Noel
Designer: Maria Friedrich
Cartography: Mary Firth

Printed in China

On the cover: Moss drapes down from the oaks lining the entrance to Magnolia Plantation off Ashley River Road in South Carolina's Low Country.

On the title pages, main: The gardens at Magnolia Plantation date to the early 1700s. Opened to the public after the Civil War, they are the oldest man-made public attraction in America.

On the title pages, inset: The antebellum grandeur of the R̶ ̶ ̶ ̶ ̶ ̶ ̶ ̶ ̶ ̶ ̶ ̶ ̶ ̶ ̶ ̶ ̶ ̶ ̶ ̶ ̶ ̶ ̶ ir-case and inviting, white-columned porch.

CONTENTS

INTRODUCTION

FACING PAGE:
The sun rises over the beach on Pawleys Island, one of the oldest summer getaways for tourists on the East Coast.

ABOVE:
A cotton boll "in bloom" at The Columns, a plantation that is still in operation near Florence in South Carolina's Pee Dee region.

South Carolina's backroads beckon and tempt. They lead through a land of startling contrasts—to regions so different in geography, culture, and temperament that it's hard to believe they exist in the same state. A single day's drive can take you from the waterfalls and misty green forests of the Blue Ridge Mountains through the rolling peach orchards of the upstate piedmont, past the vast cotton fields of the eastern piedmont, to the moss-draped oaks and wildlife-filled salt marshes of the Low Country.

Many people first encounter South Carolina along the warm, sandy shores of Myrtle Beach or the other beaches of the glorious Grand Strand. Although this is one of the state's most visited regions, it still offers more than its share of backroad surprises, such as the golden tidal marshes of Murrells Inlet; the wild, windswept dunes of Huntington Beach State Park; and the green, blossom-filled beauty of Brookgreen Gardens.

Farther south lies the romantic and mysteriously lovely Low Country, named for the maze of Sea Islands and stunning tidal marshlands that extend for miles inland, rarely rising more than forty feet above sea level. In the heart of this amazing landscape, the historic gem of Beaufort sits in antebellum splendor at the edge of the Intracoastal Waterway. Beaufort is a favorite with Hollywood. This is where Forrest Gump lived and where the thirty-something friends jogged through the morning mist in *The Big Chill.*

Between the coast and the mountains lies the vast piedmont region. This part of the state is one of the least explored by visitors. But it won't stay that way for long as more and more people discover its charms. The backroads of this region travel past historic plantations and vast fields of cotton, tobacco, and soybeans. Here, blackwater rivers regularly overflow their banks, creating flooded cypress and tupelo swamps that are bursting with life.

Some of South Carolina's most beautiful rural landscapes are found in the western piedmont, which lies between Columbia and the mountains. Here, the backroads travel through the gently rolling countryside, past horse farms and lush peach orchards. Main Street America is thriving here in perfectly preserved historic towns like Chester, Cheraw, and Abbeville, where turn-of-the-twentieth-century brick buildings line broad sidewalks and where the residents still stop to chat with each other on their way to the hardware store or ice cream parlor.

The western piedmont is also lake country. Everyone here, it seems, has a boat, and on any summer day, the sparkling blue waters of Lakes Hartwell, Murray, Greenwood, and Russell (to name a few) churn as fishing and pleasure boats of all varieties head out to find their favorite pristine coves and fishing holes.

In the far western end of the state, the Appalachian escarpment rises dramatically some two thousand feet above the rolling foothills. This is a small part of South Carolina, but what it lacks in size, it more than makes up for in stunning vistas and spectacularly scenic backroads that trace serpentine lines upward into the ancient mountains that the Cherokee called

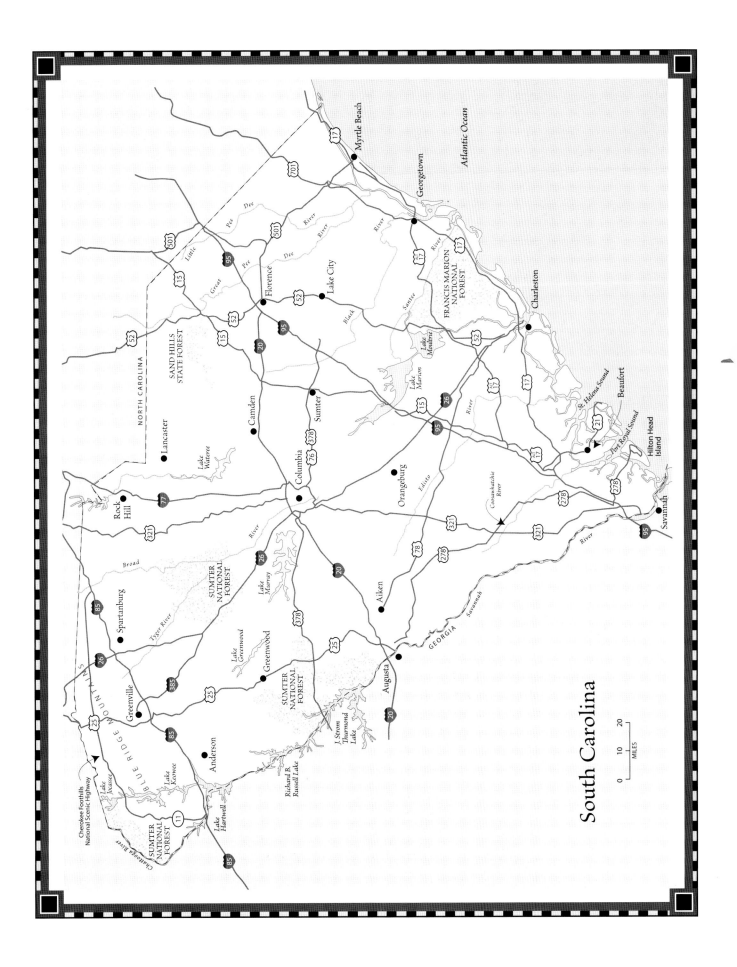

South Carolina

Pawleys Island is noted for the elegant beach homes that line the sandy shore.

Fresh-picked peaches fill wicker peck baskets at a roadside fruit stand near Belton.

The Burt Stark Mansion is in historic Abbeville, where Confederate President Jefferson Davis held his last war cabinet meeting on May 2, 1865. Today, the mansion is open to the public.

Eastatoe Valley is one of the pretty, hidden valleys, called "coves" in mountain parlance, that are found throughout the Blue Ridge Mountains.

"the great blue hills of God." From a distance, the mist-filled valleys indeed look blue. Up close, though, this is a vibrantly green world of deep forests, rushing rivers, and tumbling cascades with names like Issaqueena, Wildcat, and Twin Falls. These hills are home to the raging Chattooga River, where rafters and kayakers challenge the roaring whitewater rapids made famous in the movie *Deliverance*. And hidden here are emerald valleys where horses graze in lush meadows and water-powered mills still grind corn and wheat just as they did a century ago.

South Carolina has never been content simply to allow history to happen. Time and again—through innovation, daring, sweat, and too often blood—it has forged a story more dramatic than fiction. The marshlands of the Low Country were one of the first places in the colonies to be settled. The rice plantations that took hold here were fabulously successful, producing wealth on a level that rivaled that of the great maritime merchants of New England or the tobacco barons of Virginia. Wealthy, privileged, and highly educated, South Carolinians were leaders in the early years of a young America. It was here that many of the most important and decisive battles of the Revolutionary War were fought. And many scholars have called South Carolina the state where the Confederacy began and ended. Today, from the elegantly restored plantations of the Low Country to the historic battlefields of Camden and Kings Mountain, much of this history has been preserved.

Creating *Backroads of South Carolina* involved a year of research and traveling more than 10,000 miles of country roads and rural routes of every description. We have chosen some of our favorite routes for this book, but we know that one book could not contain all of the intriguing possibilities for exploring this fascinating state. So while exploring one of these byways, if you find your muse luring you down a backroad of your own choosing, go for it! One thing that makes South Carolina's backroads so compelling is that they serve up a constant stream of unexpected delights. From a boiled-peanut vendor in Pendleton and broom-making shop in Boykin to the captivating loveliness of a cypress swamp and the spectacular vistas of the Blue Ridge Mountains, the backroads of South Carolina lead to adventure, beauty, and discovery. See you there!

INDIGO, RICE, AND SOUTH CAROLINA'S FIRST GOLDEN AGE

Unlike pioneers in other parts of America, the first settlers who arrived in South Carolina from the West Indies had skills, money, and a plan. They were successful planters looking for more land and opportunities, and one of their first goals was to determine which crops could be successfully grown here.

Early on, they experimented with crops that they were familiar with from the islands. Some, like sugar cane, quickly proved unsuited to the climate, while others, such as rice, flourished in the tidal marshlands surrounding Charleston. Indigo also flourished, and when Britain's other sources of indigo were disrupted, South Carolina became the primary supplier of indigo to the British Empire. Indigo and rice could be raised efficiently together, as indigo required tending in summer and rice required tending the other three seasons, so one workforce could plant, tend, and harvest both crops.

It took an acre of land to produce eighty pounds of indigo. The process for extracting the blue dye from the plant and processing it is largely credited to Eliza Lucas Pinckney, an intelligent and enterprising woman who grew up in Antigua and was educated in London before arriving in South Carolina. Pinckney became manager of her father's plantations at age sixteen when he was recalled to active military service in Antigua during Britain's war with Spain.

After the Revolutionary War, the British refused to buy indigo from the colonies, and indigo virtually disappeared as a cash crop, leaving rice as the dominant economic engine in South Carolina. Rice production proved to be very labor intensive, however. To clear the land of trees, build ditches and dikes, as well as plant and harvest hundreds or even thousands of acres of rice every year took vast amounts of human effort. The planters relied on slave labor and the rapidly growing and enormously profitable slave trade that had served them well in the West Indies.

Rice was in great demand in northern Europe both for human consumption and as cattle feed. As Carolina rice developed a reputation for being superior to rice from Asia, prices rose and the rice planters became more prosperous. The perfecting of tidal flooding techniques and the invention of the mechanical rice mill dramatically improved per-acre production and boosted the profitability of rice into the stratosphere. Lawyers, ship captains, blacksmiths, and anyone who could afford to began purchasing land and planting rice.

Rice went through several boom-and-bust cycles, but by the 1840s, many large growers were producing as much as a million pounds annually, earning up to $40,000, or about thirty-five times the average worker's income. The planters built grand houses, entertained lavishly, traveled to Europe, and returned to buy more land to put into rice production.

With the Civil War and the emancipation of the slaves, rice production shifted to Alabama, Texas, and other locations, and the rice culture of coastal South Carolina came to an end. All that remains today are the few dazzlingly elegant homes and vast tracts of Low Country wetlands, some of which, like those that make up the ACE Basin National Wildlife Refuge, have been allowed to return to their wild state for the preservation of nature and the pleasure of generations to come.

After the Civil War, South Carolina's rice production plummeted because the slaves had been freed. Library of Congress

PART I

CHARLESTON AND THE LOW COUNTRY

FACING PAGE:

In the 1830s, John Grimke Drayton promised his homesick northern wife that he would turn their plantation into "a paradise on earth." The result became the magnificent gardens of Magnolia Plantation.

ABOVE:

A roadside stand on Edisto Island offers traditional sweetgrass baskets woven by Gullah women. After the Civil War, much of the land on the Sea Islands was deeded to newly freed slaves. Known as the Gullahs, they developed a unique language and culture that endures today.

Stunningly beautiful and mysteriously compelling, the low-lying marshlands and Sea Islands of South Carolina's southern coastline present one of the most unique landscapes in America. Seen from the air, the land seems to melt slowly into the sea, and the hundreds of channels of water that coil endlessly through tidal marshes look like the circulatory system of some vast waterborne creature. The marshes are one of the greatest nurseries for wildlife in North America, home to an abundance of songbirds, wading birds, ducks, and a host of other waterfowl. The shoreline teems with deer, fox, and raccoons, while alligators glide stealthily through the still black waters.

Richly historic towns like Charleston and Beaufort are graced with elegant white-columned antebellum homes that overlook the water. Beaufort is the epitome of a gracious southern small town, with oak-shaded narrow streets lined with lovely nineteenth-century homes and a four-block-long Main Street that offers a potpourri of galleries, boutiques, fine restaurants, and old-time ice cream parlors. The waterfront overlooks the Intracoastal Waterway, and the wide harbor walk is lined with two-person porch swings where you can sit on a warm afternoon and watch the boats go by.

Along the coast, on Sea Islands with names like Edisto, St. Helena, and Daufuskie, small rural lanes lead below green oak and pecan canopies to ancient rice plantations, small timeless settlements, and sandy beaches. Here and there, you can find roadside stands where Gullah women sell their intricately crafted sweetgrass baskets. These islands were settled by Gullahs—freed slaves who developed their own unique language and culture. Elsewhere on the islands, you can find untrammeled sand beaches and weatherworn docks where shrimp boats await the next tide to head out and harvest the wealth of the sea.

SOUTHERN CHARM AND THE SEA ISLANDS
BEAUFORT TO HUNTING ISLAND BEACH

ROUTE 1

Follow U.S. Highway 21 east 18 miles from Beaufort to Hunting Island State Park.

If there is a poster town for Southern charm, it is Beaufort, which graces the banks of South Carolina's Intracoastal Waterway with antebellum grandeur. In his book *Around America*, legendary news anchor Walter Cronkite says that "the sweet smell of the South, of camellias and azaleas, clings to Beaufort's ancient and historic buildings."

Halfway between Charleston and Savannah, Beaufort is best experienced along the waterfront, where a row of inviting porch-type swings offers a great place to sit and gaze at the boat-filled marina and watch the constant parade of yachts, shrimp boats, barges, and runabouts traveling the waterway.

In spite of Beaufort's charm, tourism has not discovered the town as much as you might think. A walk along Bay Street turns up galleries and gift shops, but no T-shirt shops or chain stores. In fact, the entire downtown has been designated by the National Trust for Historic Preservation as a historic district because Beaufort is one of the only Southern towns occupied, rather than destroyed, by Union troops during the Civil War. The town's restaurants cater as much to locals as visitors. Plum's offers excellent sandwiches, a view

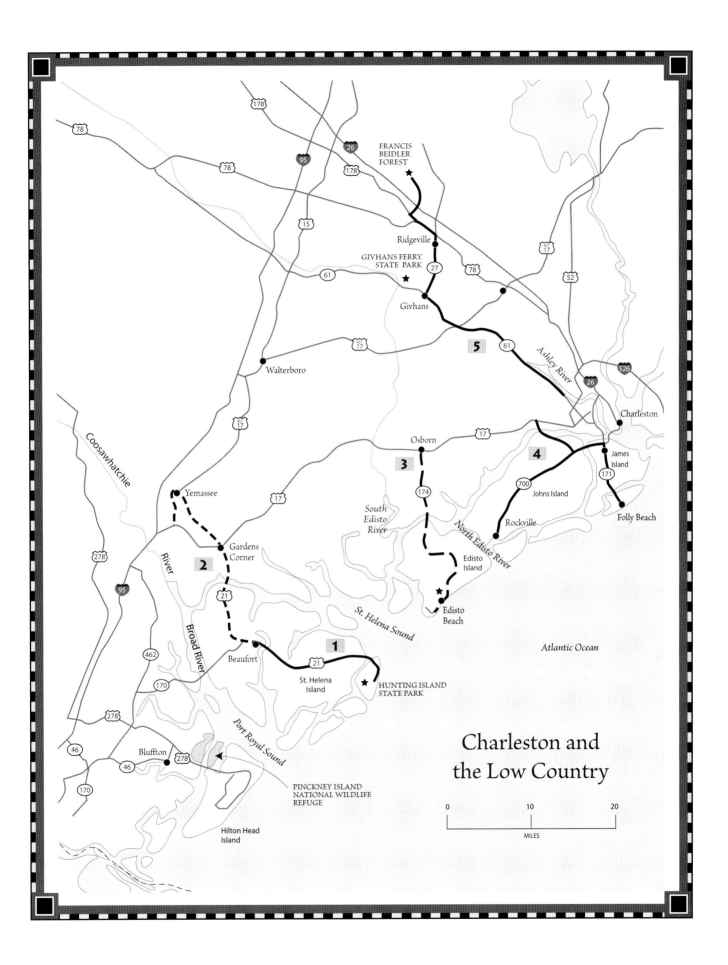

Charleston and
the Low Country

FRANCIS
BEIDLER
FOREST

Ridgeville

GIVHANS FERRY
STATE PARK

Givhans

Walterboro

Osborn

Charleston

James
Island

3

5

4

Johns Island

Folly Beach

Rockville

South
Edisto
River

Edisto
Island

Yemassee

Gardens
Corner

2

Coosawhatchie

Edisto
Beach

Atlantic Ocean

St. Helena Sound

North Edisto River

Ashley River

1

Beaufort

St. Helena
Island

HUNTING ISLAND
STATE PARK

Broad River

River

Bluffton

PINCKNEY ISLAND
NATIONAL WILDLIFE
REFUGE

Port Royal Sound

Hilton Head
Island

0   10   20

MILES

The shrimp boat Tide Runner *basks in the late afternoon sunlight that washes across the salt marshes of St. Helena Island near Beaufort.*

A heron wades amid the sunset reflections of a tidal salt marsh on St. Helena Island. Home to an abundance of birds and wildlife, the marshes of the Low Country are one of the most productive natural environments on earth.

One of the charms of exploring South Carolina's Low County is finding charming shops, like this one on St. Helena Island, in unexpected places.

of the water, and fresh seafood dinners and homemade ice cream that are the stuff of legend.

Farther up the street, you can stop and tour the historic Verdier House. Its original owner, John Mark Verdier, was typical of the risk-taking entrepreneurial colonists who helped create the American economic powerhouse of the early nineteenth century. In 1790, Verdier was a prosperous merchant exporting rice to England. Five years later, he was pacing in debtor's prison. Yet just a few years after that, he had not only recovered, but he was flourishing, making a small fortune in the Sea Islands cotton trade. Around 1804, he began building his Bay Street home, the largest and finest house in the town at the time. Today, the house is graciously decorated with period furniture that reflects the era when Verdier entertained the richest and most powerful families of South Carolina. According to local legends, the Marquis de Lafayette, who served under and was a lifelong friend of General George Washington, made a speech to the people of Beaufort from the porch of the Verdier House during his triumphant return to the United States in 1825.

Many more fine homes can be seen in a walking tour of Beaufort's lovely, tree-shaded streets, especially in the area known as Old Point, a lovely enclave of historic homes located just north of Woods Bridge. Here, elegant Greek Revival homes stand in antebellum splendor on immaculate lawns. Among the houses that you'll find are Tidalholm, the house featured in the movie *The Big Chill* (page 28), and an elegant home built by John Verdier's oldest son.

When you are ready to take leave of Beaufort's gracious ambiance, U.S. Highway 21 leads to a very different world as it heads east across Lady's Island to St. Helena Island. Here, fingers of water reach deep into the land, offering a safe haven for the shrimp boats that work the fertile waters of Low Country bays and marshes. Shortly after reaching the island, the highway passes working shrimp-boat docks. The little seafood shop nearby offers some of the freshest shrimp and fish in the region. If you'd rather have your lunch cooked for you, step across the road to the Shrimp Shack and try one of its legendary shrimp burgers.

St. Helena Island is still home to a large population of Gullahs—descendents of freed African slaves who developed their own language and culture—and the Penn Center on St. Helena is one of the best places to learn about these fascinating people and early African-American life. The center includes four galleries of photographs and artifacts of the Penn Center School, one of the first schools founded for freed slaves in 1862. Dr. Martin Luther King Jr. met with Penn School staff to discuss their role in the successful 1963 March on Washington and is said to have written the first draft of his "I Have a Dream" speech here.

A few miles farther east on the highway, fresh sea breezes blow through the palmetto trees that stand in heavy thickets on Hunting Island. Rising above the canopy of dark green fronds is the graceful 126-foot-high black-and-white tower of Hunting Island Lighthouse. Built in 1875, the current

Surrounded by golden marshes, St. Helena is a beautiful sea island that lies along the Low Country coastline near Beaufort. It is also home to the largest population of the unique culture known as Gullah.

Once, the sea islands of the Low Country were famous for their production of rice and cotton. After the Civil War, communities on these islands grew quickly as newly freed slaves sought safe havens where they could grow crops, fish, and live in peace. Plantation owners, who considered the low, marshy islands to be inferior, had no problem selling the land to the newly freed slaves.

Isolated from the outside world, these hardy, self-sufficient people developed customs and a language all their own. Technically, Gullah is not a language but a Creole dialect that is based on English combined with African words and phrasing. In Gullah, the biblical phrase "blessed are the meek for they shall inherit the earth" is spoken as "dey bless fa true, dem wa ain tink dey mo den wa dey da, cause all de whole wol gwine blongst ta um."

After World War II, the Gullah culture came under pressure as young men left their communities to seek work and developers began buying land on neighboring islands. Today, there is a resurgence of interest in Gullah culture. With more than ten thousand Gullah residents, St. Helena Island is the hub of Gullah culture, and the Penn Center is the historic and cultural center of Gullah life.

Begun as the first school for newly freed slaves in 1862, Penn Center now operates as an institute with a mandate to preserve and protect the history and culture of the Sea Islands and Gullah way of life. If you are lucky enough to be here in the second week of November, the Penn Center hosts a four-day Gullah festival when all are welcome to come and sample Gullah food, music, and culture. (Beaufort hosts its own Gullah festival in May.)

Today, in addition to farming and fishing, the Gullahs are famous for producing fine crafts, including lovely baskets that are intricately woven from sea grass. Roadside stands where Gullah families sell their baskets and other crafts can often be seen along the roads around Charleston and on the Sea Islands. The Penn Center maintains a gift shop where Gullah crafts can be purchased.

These scenes of Gullah cotton production near Beaufort were drawn by an artist traveling with General William T. Sherman's troops. The images appeared in Frank Leslie's Illustrated Newspaper, *a New York–based competitor of* Harper's Weekly. Library of Congress

The beach at Hunting Island State Park is receding as tidal currents move sand from here to other places along the shore. As the beach erodes, trees fall victim to the surf.

Built in 1875, the Hunting Island Lighthouse was constructed using cast-iron sections that could be easily dismantled and moved inland as the island eroded.

lighthouse replaced one constructed in 1859. The original was blown to pieces by Confederate troops who didn't want the Union navy to take control of it. Today, the lighthouse is open to the public. By climbing to the top of it, you'll get a spectacular view across the neighboring marshes and Sea Islands.

A short distance from the lighthouse, the fine sandy ribbon of Hunting Island Beach stretches along the coast. Like many sea islands, Hunting Island is shrinking—actually migrating—as ocean currents scoop sand away from this stretch of shore and deposit it elsewhere along the coast. It is not unusual to come across trees lying on the beach where they have fallen as the beach moves relentlessly inland driven by the forces of wind and tide.

The beach's erosion is not a new phenomenon. Back in 1875, the light-house was rebuilt with preformed panels of cast iron so that it could be dismantled and moved as the island eroded. And in 1889, workers did exactly that, moving it a mile and a quarter inland. Over the years, Hunting Island has continued to erode, and today the lighthouse that was once far inland stands less than a hundred yards from the rolling ocean surf.

The Maxcy-Rhett House is just one of many historical antebellum homes in Beaufort. It is also known as the Secession House because one-time owner Edmund Rhett held many meetings discussing Southern independence here. Library of Congress

Ruins and Rivers
Beaufort, Old Sheldon Church, Tomotley Plantation, and Frampton Plantation

U.S. Highway 21 is one of those wonderful roads that leads away from the hubbub of coastal development and into a landscape that is both surprising and mysterious—where the ghosts of South Carolina's past thrive in the quiet woods and wetlands.

It's easy to imagine otherworldly spirits at the ruins of Old Sheldon Church, but if they are here, they are gentle spirits indeed. This is a tranquil space shaded by two-hundred-year-old oaks ethereally draped with Spanish moss. In the center stands the shell of the old church, whose graceful brick arches and columns stand in defiance of time and turmoil. The sense of peace here is profound. Birds glide through the sun-dappled forest, and ancient graves dot the grounds.

Within the walls of the church is the tomb of William Bull. A member of the Colonial House of Commons from 1706 to 1719, Bull helped build the first church, known as Prince William's Parish Church, between 1745 and 1755. It was a glorious building whose elegant columns and pediments marked it as one of the first Greek Revival buildings in America.

But in 1779, as the Revolutionary War arrived in the Low Country, legend has it that the British discovered Patriot forces had used the church to store munitions, and they burned it to the ground. More than forty years passed before the church was rebuilt, and it stood for another four decades until the end of the Civil War, when troops under the command of General William Tecumseh Sherman burned it again. Today, the hauntingly beautiful ruins stand as a touchstone for the local community and still serve as a place of worship. A well-attended service is held here every spring, on the second Sunday after Easter.

Just north of Sheldon Church are the gates of Tomotley Plantation. The estate is private, but there is room to park across the road, so you can get out and admire one of the finest oak allées in America. The sandy lane that leads to the plantation is shaded on both sides by huge spreading oaks festooned with moss. The plantation's existence was first recorded in 1698, but it was not until 1820 that the rows of live oaks were planted by Patience Wise Blackett Izard. By the 1860s, the plantation encompassed more than 1,400 acres, which were worked by 138 slaves. In 1865, Sherman's troops rode in and burned the main plantation house, but left the magnificent oaks unharmed. The current house, barely visible at the end of the allée, was built in 1910.

Nearby Yemassee is a classic South Carolina crossroads town and was named for the Indian tribe that once dominated this area. In 1715, the Yamassee struck terror into the hearts of colonists as they waged a bloody war across the state. Things are considerably more peaceful in modern-day Yemassee, though.

ROUTE 2

From Beaufort, follow U.S. Highway 21 north 15 miles to Gardens Corner, where you'll veer west on the combined U.S. Highway 17/21 to the intersection of Cotton Hall Road. Turn north (right) on Cotton Hall Road and continue to Old Sheldon Church. After visiting the church, continue north on Cotton Hall Road, bear left at the intersection with Old Sheldon Church Road, and go a half mile farther north to Tomotley Plantation. After admiring the oak allées, return to Old Sheldon Church Road and turn north (left) to Yemassee. From Yemassee, take the combined U.S. Highway 17A/21 south until it merges with the combined U.S. 17/21. Follow the highway southeast a short distance to the Low Country Visitors Center (Frampton Plantation).

In the eighteenth and nineteenth centuries, plantation owners demonstrated their wealth by creating grand entrances to their homes. One of the finest of its kind in the Low Country, this stately allée of live oaks graces the entrance to Tomotley Plantation near Beaufort.

Sheldon Church has been destroyed twice, once by the British during the Revolutionary War and once by the Union Army during the Civil War. Today, the tranquil ruins are a favorite place for weddings and family gatherings.

Horse-drawn carriages take tourists along the historic streets of Beaufort, where elegant antebellum homes are a symbol of the town's early prosperity.

The waterfront in Beaufort faces the Intracoastal Waterway. Comfortable two-person swings placed along the walkway make for a pleasant place to sit and watch the endless parade of yachts and working boats go by.

HOLLYWOOD MEETS THE LOW COUNTRY

The beauty of the Low Country and antebellum Beaufort in particular have made this region of South Carolina one of the most popular movie-making destinations in America. In recent years, more than twenty movies have been filmed here.

One of the best known and most famous is *Forrest Gump* (1993). Several areas in and around Beaufort served as sets for the film. The scene in which Forrest's friend Bubba dies in a Vietnam jungle was shot on nearby Hunting Island, and Forrest's cross-country run includes a jog across Beaufort's lovely Woods Bridge.

Sandra Bullock and Ben Affleck romanced here in the 1998 comedy *Forces of Nature*, and Will Smith was often seen around town during the filming of *The Legend of Bagger Vance* (1990), much of which was filmed at nearby Colleton River Plantation.

Locals report that Barbara Streisand had to be lured to Beaufort before the filming of *Prince of Tides* (1991), which was based on the best-selling novel by famous local author Pat Conroy. Once here, however, she fell in love with the town's historic charm and she reportedly visited Plums frequently during filming to sample its homemade ice cream.

But perhaps no movie scene is more linked with the charm of Beaufort than the one in *The Big Chill* (1983) where the friends jog together through the town in the early morning mist. The famous house featured in the film is actually Tidalholm on Laurence Street in Old Point. The elegant Italianate house, built in 1853 by Edgar Fripp, was also used as a set in the Robert Duvall movie *The Great Santini* (1979), another movie based on a book by Pat Conroy.

Other movies made in and around Beaufort include:

- *Gone Fishing*, released in 1997 and starring Danny Glover, Joe Pesci, and Rosanna Arquette.
- *The War*, released in 1994 and starring Kevin Costner and Elijah Wood.
- *Something to Talk About*, released in 1995 and starring Julia Roberts, Dennis Quaid, and Robert Duvall.
- *The Jungle Book*, released in 1994 and starring Jason Scott Lee, Sam Neill, and John Cleese.
- *The General's Daughter*, released in 1999 and starring John Travolta and Madeleine Stowe.
- *Rules of Engagement*, released in 2000 and starring Tommy Lee Jones and Samuel L. Jackson.

The hottest action is at Harold's Country Club. Harold's is one of the most unusual restaurants in the Low Country, if not in America. It started back in the early 1970s when a local gas station owner named Harold Peeples wanted to increase the income from his gas station and decided to open a restaurant in the service bays of the gas station. On weekends, he cleared out the cars being repaired, scrubbed the floors, and set up tables.

Today, the cars and the service bays are gone, but the spirit of Harold's has not only lived on, but thrived. Only one meal choice is served on any evening. On Wednesdays, it's hamburgers and hot dogs. Thursday is potluck night, and on Friday night, chicken wings are offered. The most popular night is Saturday (so popular, advance reservations are required), when Harold's serves thick, juicy, rib-eye steaks.

Particularly on Saturday nights, the crowd at Harold's is, to put it mildly, eclectic. On our recent visit, we overheard one regular say, "Harold's attracts the most amazing cross-section of humanity I've ever seen in one place." And it's true. Families with young kids rub elbows with investment bankers, tattooed bikers, grannies, truck drivers, hunters, drug store cowboys, and marine drill sergeants. From time to time, famed movie director Joel Silver shows up with a movie star or two in tow. Martha Stewart has eaten here, as have Mel Gibson, Nick Nolte, and Tom Berenger.

Harold's decor is somewhere between that of a redneck hunting cabin and a 1930s-era gas station. Either way, Harold's never loses its warm, family-friendly feeling. When the doors open for seating, you get in line, and the ladies of Harold's fork over thick, wonderfully seasoned steaks and baked potatoes, then point you toward the salad bar. Diners belly up to long wooden tables and get to know their neighbors. If you don't like people and the best of Southern quirkiness, then Harold's is not for you. But you should still go once, just to say you did.

From Yemassee, the combined U.S. Highway 17A/21 heads south for several miles to another gracious plantation home that now serves as the Lowcountry Visitors Center and Museum. The house is located on land originally settled by the Frampton family. After John Frampton's first house was burned by the Union army, he rebuilt this attractive Greek Revival home in 1868. Behind the house stand earthworks that once defended a line of the Charleston and Savannah Railway.

The gardenlike grounds are attractive, and ancient oaks shade the house front and rear. The inside of the house contains a combination tourist information center, local history museum, and attractive gift shop. In all, it's a pleasant place to take a break and learn about the area before you head off to explore Beaufort or Hilton Head Island.

When Sherman's troops rode into Tomotley Plantation in 1865, they burned the main house but left the magnificent allée of oaks standing. Voyageur Press Archives

The view from Hilton Head Island, looking across the Intracoastal Waterway to the pristine Pinckney Island National Wildlife Refuge, is spectacular. The refuge's 10,000 acres of protected wetlands are home to a dazzling variety of birds and wildlife.

Birds roost on a channel marker at sunset along the Edisto River near Edisto Island.

History and Mystery on the Last Sea Island
ACE Basin National Wildlife Refuge to Edisto Island

Route 3

From its junction with U.S. Highway 17, follow South Carolina Highway 174 (Edisto Road) south to S-10-55 (Willtown Road). Turn west (right) on Willtown Road to the ACE Basin National Wildlife Refuge. To complete the route, return to Highway 174 and turn south to Edisto Island and Edisto Beach.

On a point of land at the juncture of the Edisto and Dawho rivers stands an elegant antebellum plantation house, one of very few in this area to have survived the ravages of time and war. This is the Grove Plantation, and its peaceful, oak-shaded grounds are the doorway to the largest expanse of pristine tidal wetlands left in America.

The Grove was built in 1828 by plantation owner George Morris. When he died of malaria in 1834, his wife, Maria, took control of the rice plantation over the objections of her family, who thought running a plantation was unladylike. Under Maria's management, the plantation not only became profitable, but it also thrived, allowing her to pay off her husband's debts and begin new business ventures. Her only failure came when she tried to turn the plantation over to her free-wheeling, hard-drinking son.

George Morris Jr. had little interest in running the plantation and it quickly sank again into debt. One day, George's horse came home alone, and when a search party was sent out to find him, they discovered his body hanging from a tree. Whether it was suicide or the settling of a local vendetta remains a mystery to this day.

The Civil War brought hard times to the area, and around 1890, rice prices began collapsing as cheaper rice from Alabama and Texas flooded the market. Eventually, the Grove, like many other large Low Country plantations, was sold to a wealthy sportsman, who used it as a hunting retreat. As development began to encroach on the wild areas of the Low Country, many conservationists began to voice the need to preserve as much of the wetlands as possible. Soon a coalition of conservation groups, including the Nature Conservancy, Ducks Unlimited, and the U.S. Fish and Wildlife Service, formed a unique partnership with numerous Low Country landholders, creating the ACE Basin National Wildlife Refuge.

"ACE" refers to the three most important rivers in the area: the Ashepoo, Combahee, and Edisto. In all, the ACE Basin National Wildlife Refuge protects more than 11,500 acres. Like the Grove Plantation, much of this land was originally rice plantations. Throughout the region, the old rice dikes have been repaired, new ponds have been built, and the fields are seasonally flooded to create habitat for migrating ducks and waterfowl, including mallards, pintails, shovelers, and widgeon, who call the marsh home from spring through fall.

Yet the marshes and low-lying woodlands of the ACE Basin teem with wildlife at any time of the year. Wood storks, egrets, and herons wade in the still backwaters. Songbirds, including painted buntings, bluebirds, warblers, and finches, inhabit the reserve by the thousands. Alligators cruise silently through the dark waters, while river otters and raccoons hunt along the banks. Deer, fox, rabbits, and squirrels inhabit the meadows and woods.

Today, the Grove is the headquarters for the wildlife refuge. Visitors can tour several rooms inside the historic plantation house. The lower floor features displays that relate the natural and human history of the ACE Basin. Beyond the house, several hiking trails lead through the marsh and woodlands and along the dikes of the reconstructed rice ponds, offering a great way to experience the beauty of the marshes.

Continuing along U.S. 17 south of the wildlife refuge, you cross the gracefully curved bridge that spans the Dawho River. The view as you cross is spectacular, with vast expanses of green or golden salt marsh grasses and channels of sapphire blue water that stretch to the horizon. Driving onto Edisto Island, you enter a world apart, one of the least spoiled of all the Sea Islands. Time and seasons seem to pass more slowly here. The island is crisscrossed with narrow sandy lanes that create sun-dappled tunnels through emerald stands of ancient, moss-bearded oaks. Edisto is home to one of the largest populations of Gullah people in the Low Country, and here and there casual roadside stands offer the delicate and incredibly intricate sweetgrass baskets woven by the Gullah women.

Just about the only man-made attraction on the island is the small but fascinating Edisto Island Museum, which features displays and artifacts from the island's long history. The earliest artifacts include fossils, shark teeth, and whale bones from the Precambrian era five hundred million years ago, when this region was covered by a shallow sea. More modern collections include items from the early days of the island's European settlement—displays of toys, farm implements, and household utensils from the eighteenth and nineteenth centuries.

The island's coastline provides the perfect habitat for South Carolina's state tree, the palmetto, and some of the tallest palmettos anywhere are found on the northwest tip of the island in Edisto Beach State Park. The park is even better known for the loggerhead turtles that come ashore here each summer to lay their eggs in the sand. South Carolina is the nesting area for about 850 of the 14,000 loggerhead turtles that nest in the southeastern United States.

The park protects a nearly flawless mile and a half of wild Atlantic sand beach that is considered to be one of South Carolina's best shelling destinations. The coast must have been just as seductive to peoples of centuries past, for archaeological evidence shows that Native Americans camped here on a regular basis. The park contains a sixty-foot-high shell mound, or midden, that attests to the bounty from the sea that people enjoyed as early as 2500 B.C.

Considered to be one of the oldest and largest live oaks in the Low Country, Angel Oak is estimated to be up to 1,400 years old. The oak and the small park surrounding it are one of the most popular destinations on Johns Island.

The Low Country is a kayaker's paradise, so much so that a popular kayak festival is held every spring at James Island County Park near Charleston.

Pleasure boats ride calmly near the private docks that line the tidal marshes of Folly Island near Charleston.

The elegant marsh-side cottages at James Island County Park are regularly rented by families and groups on vacation.

Of the 940 square miles in Beaufort County, South Carolina, over one third, about 330 square miles, are tidal marshlands.

Marshes come in many varieties—freshwater marshes, salt marshes, and tidal or brackish marshes. The marshes in South Carolina's Low Country are mostly salt and tidal marshes that are created as freshwater from slow-moving inland rivers approaches the coast and mixes with the ocean saltwater brought in by the twice-daily tides. Generally speaking, the closer the marsh is to the sea, the higher its salt content will be.

The tall, tough cord grasses of the marsh are the foundation of its ecosystem and create tons of nutrients as they decay. These nutrients feed the microorganisms that are at the base of the food chain. Twice a day, the tides roll in and lift plant matter from the marsh bottom, stirring up nutrients that feed microorganisms, which in turn create food for small marine animals, fish, and shrimp. The tides also bring in the porpoises and larger fish that feed on the shrimp and small fish.

The grasses create an almost impenetrable network of roots and stalks, which form a protected nursery for shrimp and crabs, as well as young fish like mullet, menhaden, flounder, and drum. The shrimp, spawned offshore, go through ten larval stages and enter the marshes as young adults. They ride the tides upward to feed in the grasses, and they return to the marsh bottom as the tide retreats. In summer, the shrimp grow up to two inches a month, and as they grow, they move to deeper water nearer the coast.

With its floor of seemingly bottomless soft, gooey pluff mud and vast beds of razor-sharp oysters, the marsh is a magnificent fortress for the birthing of life, and the marshes of South Carolina's Low Country are some of the most fertile and productive ecosystems on the planet. The grass hummocks, many of which have small stands of trees, are home to a wide variety of nesting birds, including clapper rails, bitterns, and moorhens. The shallows of the marsh waters near shore are the haunt of wading birds, such as great blue herons, wood storks, and egrets.

Clouds and blue sky are perfectly reflected in the tranquil waters of the tidal marshes along Bennetts Point Road in South Carolina's Low Country.

SEA ISLANDS AND ANCIENT OAKS
JOHNS ISLAND TO FOLLY BEACH

On Johns Island, where huge old oaks are common, one tree is of particular note. Experts estimate that Angel Oak was more than a thousand years old when the first European explorers landed on this marsh island, located just south of present-day Charleston, around 1670. Today, the oak's great arms, one of which is eighty-nine feet long, curve to the ground, then rise upward again.

Angel Oak's name comes not from religious origins, but from Justis Angel, who became the master of the plantation that Angel Oak grew on in 1810. The tree is beloved in the community, and through the years various social groups have taken responsibility for its care. In 1991, the city of Charleston took over maintenance and created the small park that surrounds it. Today, a steady stream of visitors arrives to walk around the tree and gaze up at the spread of its amazing canopy.

If you look closely, you'll notice that the limbs of Angel Oak are carpeted with a green growth. This is resurrection fern, an air plant that grows on large oaks and gets its nutrients from moisture in the atmosphere. Its name comes from the fact that during dry periods the fern shrivels and appears gray, dry, and dead. With the first rain shower, however, the fronds swell and open, and the fern returns to its healthy bright green state. Studies have shown that the plant can lose 97 percent of its moisture and still survive. Some experts believe that the fern could survive in its dormant state for up to a hundred years and still be "resurrected."

A few miles down Maybank Road (South Carolina Highway 700), after crossing a small body of water, you arrive on Wadmalaw Island, where you'll find the only commercial tea plantation in the United States. Not surprisingly, as you drive into the Charleston Tea Plantation, the first thing you will see are some of the hundreds of thousands of tea plants that cover much of the plantation's 127 green acres. Tea loves subtropical climes, but even so, the history of growing tea in the New World has been fraught with disasters and disappointments. In the mid-1800s, several attempts were made to grow tea in the United States, all in South Carolina.

Then, as now, the two primary challenges American tea growers had to overcome were unpredictable weather and high labor costs. In the late 1800s, Dr. Charles Shepard started a tea plantation in Summerville, South Carolina, and solved the labor problem by creating a school where the children earned their tuition by picking tea. After his death in 1915, the plantation was untended until 1960, when it was bought by the Thomas J. Lipton Company. Lipton moved the tea plants that could be saved to Wadmalaw Island. There, one of the future co-owners of the Charleston Tea Plantation addressed the labor problem in a more enlightened vein—by modifying a cotton picker

ROUTE 4

From the intersection of U.S. Highway 17 and Main Road, head south on Main Road to River Road. Take River Road southeast to Maybank Road (South Carolina Highway 700) and turn southwest. After about 3.5 miles, Maybank Road crosses Main Road. Just past the intersection, turn left onto the unpaved Angel Oak Road. Follow this road for about half a mile to Angel Oak Park. Return to Maybank Road and travel southwest to Charleston Tea Plantation and Rockville. Return and stay on Maybank Road (Highway 700) heading northeast until just across the Stono River; then turn south onto Riverland Drive to Grimball Road. Turn left (east) onto Folly Road (South Carolina Highway 171). Turn south onto Ashley Avenue and follow it to Folly Beach.

Centuries-old oaks lean over the banks of the Ashley River. Some of South Carolina's oldest and most famous plantations once prospered along the banks of this river north of Charleston.

Magnolia Plantation's old rice fields along the banks of the Ashley River are now managed as a wildlife reserve.

and tobacco harvester to create a mechanical tea picker that could pick tea as gently and quickly as five hundred workers.

Over time, the Charleston Tea Plantation thrived, becoming the official tea supplier to the White House, as well as having lucrative contracts with distributors such as Wal-Mart. But the tea market proved ever fickle and elusive, and the plantation declined once again. In 2003, it was purchased by the Bigelow Company, makers of Constant Comment and other teas. Bigelow has refurbished the tea fields and reopened the plantation for tours. Visitors can taste samples of Bigelow's American Classic Tea, which is made here; tour the tea fields; and watch the manufacturing processes from withering (which changes the tea from green to black) through final packaging.

Just minutes away, Folly Beach is one of the least commercialized beach towns in the state. Folly Beach's motto, "the Edge of America," is not so much a physical location as a state of mind—one that is warmly embraced by residents. Having eluded the aggressive gentrification that has occurred elsewhere along the coast, Folly Beach still exudes an offbeat, 1960s-era, slightly-tacky-but-friendly feel that is refreshing when so many beaches are disappearing behind an impenetrable wall of megabuck mansions. Folly Beach is also the place where George Gershwin hung out for several months in 1934 when he was writing his hit Broadway musical *Porgy and Bess*.

The island's showpiece is the thousand-foot-long pier that extends into the Atlantic. A favorite destination for fishermen, families, and sun-loving loafers, the pier offers a short walk with a great view and a chance to enjoy the salt air. The beach here is long and inviting, perfect for an extended stroll. A more pristine beach experience awaits at the south end of the island, where Ashley Avenue ends at Folly Beach County Park. A quarter-mile walk leads to the beach, where you can see the Morris Island Lighthouse standing in the waves three hundred yards offshore.

Once there were three islands between Folly Island and Sullivan's Island to the north of Charleston. A lighthouse was built on one of them in 1767 to guide ships safely into Charleston Harbor. Time and tide merged the three islands into one long island called Morris. The current lighthouse, built in 1876, was at one time surrounded by numerous buildings, including a lighthouse keeper's residence. In the late 1800s, several large jetties were built nearby to keep shifting shoals from closing Charleston Harbor. The jetties, however, caused a shift in the currents and Morris Island began eroding rapidly. Today, the island has all but vanished below the waves, and the lighthouse seemingly sits all alone in the sea.

While this area looks forlorn, two civic organizations are working hard to raise funds to restore Morris Island and preserve the lighthouse. In the meantime, the Morris Island Lighthouse remains in the domain of seagulls, a monument to the shifting sands of the Carolina coast.

ASHLEY RIVER ROAD NATIONAL SCENIC BYWAY
CHARLESTON TO FRANCIS BEIDLER FOREST

Few roads are as short in miles but long in history as the Ashley River Road. Three hundred years ago, when Charleston was little more than a backwater trading port, the land along the Ashley River had already been cleared and planted. Rice, much in demand in Europe, was the golden crop, and this stretch of the Ashley had the fertile river bottom and tidal flow that was ideal for its cultivation.

As rice brought wealth to the area, the plantation homes along the banks of the Ashley River evolved from simple farmhouses to elaborate structures that reflected the finest architectural styles of England. One of the first of these fine homes was John Drayton's spectacular Georgian-Palladian masterpiece, Drayton Hall. The house was so magnificent for its time that locals quickly dubbed it Drayton's Palace.

As you drive onto the grounds of Drayton Hall, the house comes into view, standing solitary on a vast expanse of lawn. Devoid of any mark of the modern world, the house is like a doorway into an earlier, grander age. The feeling intensifies as you take a guided tour of the house. The inside is empty, without furniture or decor, but you gradually become aware that, amazingly, nothing in this house has changed in almost three centuries. For a variety of reasons, not one generation of Draytons modernized the house; there is no plumbing, no electricity, and no fashionable additions.

Even the paint on most walls is just the second coat in nearly three hundred years. The walls, windows, moldings, and floors look just as they did when this architectural masterpiece was completed in 1742. The house offers architectural students and history buffs a unique look at colonial architecture and the lifestyles of the rich and famous in eighteenth-century South Carolina.

Beyond Drayton Hall, the Ashley River Road becomes a soothing, two-lane country byway that traces languorous curves beneath a luxurious green canopy of moss-draped live oaks. A few miles farther upriver, turn into the driveway of Magnolia Plantation. Known worldwide for its famous gardens, Magnolia Plantation, like Drayton Hall, has a history that is intimately linked with the Drayton family.

In the late 1830s, Magnolia Plantation was already more than a century old when twenty-two-year-old John Grimke Drayton learned that his older brother had been fatally wounded in a hunting accident and that he would be inheriting the estate. A few years later, he was planning to wed Julia Ewing of Philadelphia, and although they were very much in love, his bride-to-be was terrified at the prospect of living on a Southern plantation so far from the cultured world she knew in Philadelphia. So Drayton pledged to her that he would turn Magnolia into a "paradise on earth," and he began planning and constructing what would come to be one of the greatest gardens in America.

ROUTE 5

Follow South Carolina Highway 61 (Ashley River Road) northwest from Charleston. The road name changes to Farm Field Road, but it remains Highway 61. Follow it to Givhans Ferry State Park. Return south along Highway 61 to South Carolina Highway 27, where you'll head north and continue to U.S. Highway 78. Turn west (bearing right) onto U.S. 78 and continue to head west. Continue to the junction with S-18-28 (Beidler Forest Road), where you'll head north, following S-18-28 to Francis Beidler Forest.

Horses graze placidly in the meadow in front of Magnolia Plantation. The third dwelling to go up here, the house on the plantation was built in stages by John Grimke Drayton and his daughter, who added the Victorian elements.

Cypress trees cast flawless reflections in the still swamp waters of the Francis Beidler Forest.

A view from the porch of Drayton Hall, one of the first of the grand plantation homes built along the Ashley River. The wealth of the Draytons is reflected in the home's wrought-iron railings and elegant double-entry stairs.

Although Drayton's house did not survive the Civil War, his gardens did, and in the difficult years after the war, he opened them to the public. To rebuild his house, Drayton started with a modest Revolutionary-era country home he owned farther upriver. He had that house dismantled and floated downriver to be reassembled on the site of the original home. His daughter continued expanding the house, adding rooms and the Victorian cupola, which hides a water tank that once provided the house with running water.

Today, visitors to Magnolia Plantation can explore fifty acres of stunning gardens where bridges arch across cypress wetlands and lead to secret, blossom-filled green spaces. On spring days, the garden can get crowded, as visitors flock to enjoy the riot of color created by thousands of blooming azaleas and other flowers. Drayton designed his gardens in a natural style that was popular in England in the mid-1800s. The gardens begin with formal design near the house and then gradually become more free form, eventually merging with the riverside wetlands and natural environment. All five hundred acres at Magnolia Plantation are a wildlife reserve. One set of paths leads through the Audubon Swamp Garden, one of the most lovely and accessible cypress wetlands in the country.

Just a few miles upriver stands another of Ashley River Road's great plantations. At first glance, it is easy to assume that Middleton Place, like Drayton Hall, escaped the wrath of Sherman's troops. But then you realize that this fine brick home is just a modest wing of the original spectacular Jacobean mansion that once stood beside it. Indeed, the house that Henry Middleton built in 1741 was created not only to be impressive by colonial standards, but also to compare favorably to the finest country estates of England.

Along with his fine home, Middleton planned the most extensive and spectacular gardens that the colonies had ever seen. Unlike Magnolia's naturalist-style gardens that blended with the environment, Middleton took his cue from the finest formal gardens of Europe, including the gardens at the Palace at Versailles. Over ten years, bringing the vision of his gardens to life required the labor of a hundred or more slaves. Today, much of Middleton Place's original gardens still exist, including the lawn that descends in vast graceful terraces to two mirror-image ponds shaped like butterfly wings. These gardens not only are a national historic landmark, but also have been awarded the Buckley Medal, the Garden Club of America's highest honor.

Their design includes "garden rooms", such as the octagonal garden where men once practiced lawn bowling. There are quiet nooks hidden behind tall hedges that are filled with blooms and graceful Greek-inspired statuary and a magnificent, long reflection pool where swans glide in regal grandeur. Middleton Place also offers visitors a glimpse into colonial plantation life, as costumed re-enactors demonstrate period skills and crafts, such as carpentry, pottery, weaving, and barrelmaking in the stable-yard area.

A few miles north of Givhans Ferry State Park, the Francis Beidler Forest offers visitors easy access into a world that is often thought of as dark and devoid of life. Swamps are anything but lifeless, however. They are bursting with biodiversity, natural beauty, and unique forms of life that are often found nowhere else.

Once called the Four Holes Swamp, the 13,000-acre Francis Beidler Forest is owned and maintained by the National Audubon Society and contains the largest virgin stand of bald cypress and tupelo gum trees in the world. The centerpiece of the forest is a 1¾–mile-long boardwalk that meanders among the 150-foot-tall trees into the depths of the swamp.

Here among the trees, many of which are more than a thousand years old, it is easy to see the swamp as both refuge and sanctuary. It certainly was just that for Francis Marion, the Revolutionary War Patriot known as the "Swamp Fox." For Marion, who knew the swamp like the back of his hand, the magnificent wetland was an impenetrable fortress from which he could launch his lightning-fast guerilla raids against the British. It was also the place where he and a hundred or more men could quickly vanish from their pursuers. Today, the swamp offers a world far from conflict, in which brilliantly colored butterflies flit among wildflowers, and woodpeckers and songbirds create a special music among the timeless cypress cathedrals.

PART II

NORTHERN COAST AND THE GRAND STRAND

Whoever said "life's a beach" may well have had South Carolina's northern coast in mind. From the North Carolina border to Georgetown, the shore is one long beach, only occasionally broken by tidal inlets of stunning beauty. One of these is Murrells Inlet, just south of the tourist mayhem of Myrtle Beach. This lovely expanse of green marsh grasses and blue water channels is noted for the historic homes that have been preserved along the waterfront and the wealth of fine seafood restaurants that grace the small community. Famed tough-guy writer Mickey Spillane loved the fishing here and called the inlet home for over fifty years until his death in 2006.

Murrells Inlet is sheltered from the power of the sea by the wild, pristine expanse of Huntington Beach State Park. The beach vies for a visitor's attention with the lush green, flower- and sculpture-filled spaces of Brookgreen Gardens, which lie just inland. Both were gifts to the state from sculptor Anna Hyatt Huntington and her wealthy philanthropist husband, Archer. Just to the south, yet another beach stretches along the sun-washed coast. The fine sand strand of Pawleys Island is the setting for a lovely pearl-like string of million-dollar beach homes that overlook the sand and surf. Yet in spite of its upscale leanings, the island has managed to retain a friendly family feel, and locals still cast nets for shrimp among the marsh grasses that lie between the island and the mainland.

Georgetown, the largest town on the northern coast, is a very old settlement, dating to 1729 (and some scholars think this is the likely site of a settlement dating to 1526). In spite of its sometimes too-visible industrial roots, the downtown area is undergoing something of a renaissance. Where once ships loaded rice headed for the ports of Europe, today a host of waterfront shops and businesses are thriving.

Between Georgetown and Charleston lies one of the most spectacular stretches of raw, wild coastline on the eastern seaboard. Cape Romain National Wildlife Refuge stretches for more than 20 miles along the coast. A ferry takes visitors on a trip to lonely Bull Island, a remote seaside wilderness where you can hike trails that follow the marsh or stroll along the island's five miles of pristine beach, where seashells lie undisturbed and yours may well be the only footprints left in the sand.

ALONG THE UNDISCOVERED COAST
CHARLESTON TO MCCLELLANVILLE

Completed in 2005 at a cost of over $531 million, the new Arthur Ravenel Jr. Bridge is a breathtakingly beautiful celebration of form and function and a well-deserved point of pride for Charlestonians. Spanning the Cooper River between Charleston and Mount Pleasant, the bridge is supported by dramatic fan-shaped patterns of cables that drop from 174-foot-high towers, creating the illusion of triangular sails on a ship of the sea. Locals still call it the Cooper River Bridge, and at night the cables are lit by spotlights, creating an architectural spectacle that is visible from almost every part of the city.

ROUTE 6

Follow U.S. Highway 17 from historic Charleston across the bridge over Town Creek and the Cooper River and then bear right (south) on South Carolina Highway 703 (Coleman Boulevard) toward Sullivan's Island. Watch for the Y intersection and veer right (south) on Ben Sawyer Boulevard. Turn right on Middle Street and go 1.5 miles to Fort Moultrie National Monument. Return along Middle Street, jogging left for one block on Station 22 Street and then right (west) onto Highway 703 (now Jasper Boulevard), which becomes Palms Boulevard. Continue to Clyde Moultrie Dangerfield Highway (South Carolina Highway 517) and turn north onto U.S. Highway 17. Turn left on Long Point Road to Boone Hall Plantation and Charles Pinckney National Historic Site. Return to U.S. Highway 17 and head north to Sewee Visitor and Environmental Education Center, the visitor center for the Francis Marion National Forest, and Cape Romain National Wildlife Refuge. Continue north on U.S. Highway 17 to South Pinckney Road, and turn right into the historic town of McClellanville.

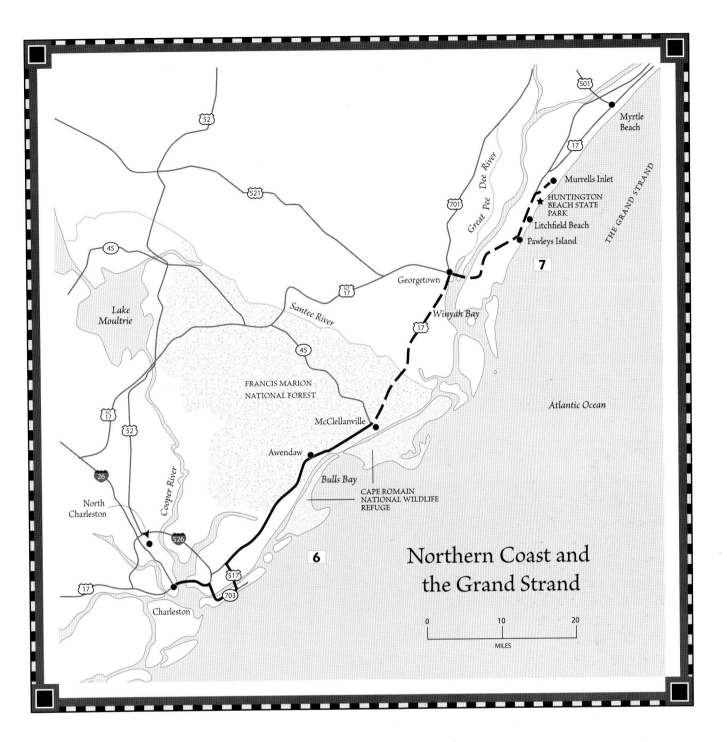

52

521

45

Lake
Moultrie

45

ALT
17

52

26

North
Charleston

Cooper River

526

517

703

Charleston

17

FRANCIS MARION
NATIONAL FOREST

Santee River

ALT
17

Georgetown

Winyah Bay

17

701

Great Pee Dee River

501

Myrtle
Beach

17

Murrells Inlet

HUNTINGTON
BEACH STATE
PARK

Litchfield Beach

Pawleys Island

7

THE GRAND STRAND

McClellanville

Awendaw

Bulls Bay

CAPE ROMAIN
NATIONAL WILDLIFE
REFUGE

Atlantic Ocean

6

Northern Coast and
the Grand Strand

0   10   20

MILES

The Charleston Battery was one of the first areas outside the walled city of Charleston to be developed. Larger home lots gave the wealthy planters and merchants of the day room to build grand houses that reflected the city's growing prosperity.

Downtown Charleston is loaded with charm, which is reflected in details like this gaslight at the Edmonston Alston House.

Stately Boone Hall Plantation lies at the end of an elegant allée of oak trees on a quiet country road a few miles outside of Charleston. Boone Hall is one of the oldest working plantations in South Carolina. It dates from 1681.

Boone Hall's historic buildings include the oldest "street" of slave cabins in America.

Less than a mile from the bridge, lovely Shem Creek is lined with a tasteful collection of homes, colorful shops, and restaurants. The docks of the busy waterway are crowded with yachts and working shrimp boats, making them a favorite subject for artists and a great place for you to spend some time strolling the waterfront or shopping. You can also drop by Coastal Expeditions, one of Charleston's oldest and most respected kayak companies. Here, you can rent a kayak for an hour or two and paddle through the lush wetlands that separate Sullivan's Island from the mainland. Coastal Expeditions also offers naturalist-led kayak tours into the vast Cape Romain National Wildlife Refuge, which lies a few miles north along the coast.

As you follow Ben Sawyer Boulevard across the tidal marshes and begin to explore Sullivan's Island, you may notice streets named Poe Avenue, Raven Street, and most importantly, Gold Bug Avenue. These names are, of course, tributes to nineteenth-century suspense writer Edgar Allen Poe, who served as a soldier here in the late 1820s. The island's sand-and-sea atmosphere must have made a lasting impression on Poe, as he used it as the setting in his treasure-hunting story *The Gold-Bug*, which was based on tales of pirate loot buried here.

Poe was stationed at Fort Moultrie. The first fort was built in 1776 out of palmetto logs. On June 28 of that year, when nine British ships attacked Charleston, the fresh, supple palm logs of the fort absorbed the blows of the British canon. The fort's own firepower eventually beat off the attack and severely damaged the British ships in the first decisive victory of the Revolutionary War. The current brick fort was built in 1809 and named after the commander of the 1776 battle, William Moultrie.

In 1860, six days after South Carolina seceded, the federal garrison at Fort Moultrie withdrew to the newer, stronger, and more defendable Fort Sumter. Confederate troops soon occupied Fort Moultrie and took part

In April of 1863, federal iron-clad ships began a massive bombardment of Fort Sumter that lasted twenty months. When it was over, the once-proud fort had been reduced to near rubble. Library of Congress

in the April bombardment of Fort Sumter, which started the Civil War. Today, Fort Moultrie is operated by the National Park Service, and visitors are welcome to tour the facility. The fort offers spectacular views of Charleston, Charleston Harbor, and lonely Fort Sumter, which stands on its own island at the harbor entrance.

On April 12, 1861, after repeated requests that Union forces under Major Robert Anderson evacuate, Confederate forces opened fire on Fort Sumter. The first volley, which was the first shot of the Civil War, came from a mortar at Fort Johnson on James Island. Library of Congress

If you love the romantic, Rhett-and-Scarlett "tomorrow-is-another-day" South as portrayed in the movie *Gone With the Wind*, it's hard to pass up a stop at Boone Hall Plantation. Ignoring the fact that the house was actually built in 1935, this plantation has enough antebellum charm for Scarlett O'Hara herself. While the house is modern, the plantation itself dates to 1681. The outbuildings include nine brick slave houses shaded by large oaks and a round brick smokehouse that may have been built as early as 1790. Throughout the summer, the gardens are a bright oasis of color, with quiet green nooks and benches that invite dawdlers. Tours of the house and grounds are available, and special events are scheduled regularly.

Nearby, the Charles Pinckney National Historic Site protects the country estate of Charles Pinckney, one of the signers of the U.S. Constitution. Pinckney was captured by the British after the fall of Charleston and remained a prisoner until 1781. He sometimes claimed he was the youngest member of the Constitutional Convention, but in fact, men younger than he had participated in the meeting. Yet Pinckney's fellow Constitutional Convention attendees praised his intellect, manners, and problem-solving skills, and agreed that Pinckney was one of the most prominent contributors to the document.

Heading north, U.S. Highway 17 passes between two of the state's most outstanding wilderness regions: the Francis Marion National Forest and the Cape Romain National Wildlife Refuge. The 64,000-acre Cape Romain National Wildlife Refuge stretches for twenty-two miles along the South Carolina coast, making it one of the largest protected coastal wetlands in America. Here, tens of thousands of wading birds, waterfowl, songbirds, and shorebirds find a permanent or seasonal home in a wild and pristine marshland that has almost no public access except by boat.

A lone surf fisherman makes a cast as the sunset sky is reflected in the wet sand at Huntington Beach State Park.

The Francis Marion National Forest and Cape Romain National Wildlife Refuge share an excellent visitor center, the Sewee Visitor and Environmental Education Center, located along Highway 17. Here you can find information on the many hiking trails available throughout the forest and refuge. The wildlife refuge currently has ongoing projects to protect loggerhead turtle nesting areas and to breed and reintroduce the rare red wolf.

If you have time, the best way to see the Cape Romain area is to take the morning ferry to spectacular and unspoiled Bulls Island. The ferry departs from a landing near the visitor center and glides through the marshlands to the mainland side of this perfect barrier island. Once you disembark, you can explore the sixteen miles of primitive roads and trails that crisscross the island or find your own starting place along the five miles of fine sand beach that faces the Atlantic. Along the beach, you can make the first (and possibly only) footprints of the day as you search for shells and seaborne treasures, with the gulls and sandpipers as your only witnesses.

The city of Charleston was also the target of constant bombardment from Union ships during the Civil War. Many of the oldest parts of the city, including the grand homes and buildings along the waterfront, were severely damaged.
Library of Congress

SALT MARSHES, SAND, AND SEA
MCCLELLANVILLE TO MURRELLS INLET

Early in 1791, John Horry was worried. His elegant new porch was not quite finished, and he was expecting an important visitor. With a little sweat, however, the last nails were driven and the columns got painted just in time for George Washington to take tea with the Horrys under the new portico of Hampton Plantation. During the visit, legend has it that Horry mentioned to Washington that he was going to cut down the big oak in front of the house. Washington, admiring the view from the front porch, urged him to preserve it. Horry took his advice, and forever after the tree has been known as the Washington Oak.

The porch was just the final touch of a massive addition and renovation that year, one that transformed the house from a modest dwelling to the grand mansion that stands today. In the early decades of the 1900s, the house slowly sank into near ruin, but in the 1940s it was carefully renovated by Archibald Rutledge, the beloved writer and poet laureate of South Carolina, who had spent his joyous boyhood at Hampton. Rutledge wrote about his experiences restoring the old house in a book he titled *A Home by the River*.

Today, Hampton Plantation is a state historic site, and the house is open for tours. Inside, the walls have been cut away in places to show construction techniques that span more than two hundred years. John Horry's eighteenth-century improvements included an elegant, large ballroom that is still the highlight of the house tour.

Hampton, like most of the plantations in the Low Country, was a rice plantation, and at one time the plantations between Georgetown and Charleston produced over half of the rice grown in America. In Georgetown, the Rice Museum presents the history of South Carolina's fabulous rice culture through interpretive displays and a large collection of historic artifacts. A new annex, the Maritime Museum Gallery, displays Brown's Ferry vessel, a fifty-foot cargo vessel that dates to 1730 and is the oldest vessel on display in the country. Also in Georgetown is the pre-Revolutionary War–era Kaminski House. This beautifully restored harbor-front home is filled with impressive antiques from the eighteenth and nineteenth centuries.

Just north of Georgetown, Pawleys Island loves to call itself "arrogantly shabby." However, there is nothing even remotely shabby about the multi-million-dollar "cottages" that line the island's lovely beach and marsh fronts, and the town founders wisely avoided arrogance by creating numerous small parking lots that allow access all along the island's lovely, sandy three-mile shore, so that mere mortals will feel welcome to enjoy the beach.

With this beach access, Pawleys has an inviting, friendly flavor that makes it a popular destination with locals and visitors alike. You reach the

ROUTE 7

Follow U.S. Highway 17 north from McClellanville and turn left (northwest) onto Rutledge Road. Go 3 miles to the entrance of Hampton Plantation State Historic Site. After visiting the plantation, return to U.S. 17 and follow it north to Georgetown. In Georgetown, turn right (southeast) on Front Street to find the Rice Museum. As you return to U.S. 17 on Front Street, you will pass the Kaminski House. Continue north on U.S. 17 and turn right (east) on South Causeway Road to Pawleys Island. Turn left (north) on Myrtle Avenue and left on North Causeway Road to return to U.S. 17. Continue north to Huntington Beach State Park and Brookgreen Gardens. Continue north and take U.S. 17's business route into Murrells Inlet.

Murrells Inlet is a famous saltwater fishing destination, and charter fishing boats are always ready to take fishermen out to try their luck.

A young alligator cruises through a freshwater wetland in Murrells Inlet.

Brookgreen Gardens is home to a world-class sculpture collection surrounded by lovely gardens and green spaces.

A group admires the whimsical Fountain of the Muses *in Brookgreen Gardens.*

island by taking one of two causeways that cross the wide salt marsh that separates the island from the mainland. During shrimp season, you'll often see locals casting nets from the bridges here. Once on the island, you can drive the length of it while admiring the lovely homes, or park and walk a stretch of the fine sand beach.

If, however, you like your beaches wild and natural, an even better walk awaits you a few miles north at Huntington Beach State Park. Entering the park, you pass through a palmetto forest and then cross a long causeway that takes you through a stunning salt marsh. The marsh is home to egrets, herons, canvasbacks, widgeon, moorhens, grebes, and a host of other wading and water birds. To the right of the causeway, a freshwater retention area is home to numerous alligators, some of impressive size. They often can be seen lying on the banks in the afternoon sun.

Near the south end of the park stands Atalaya, the Moorish-style concrete summer home of Archer Huntington and his wife, renowned sculptor Anna Hyatt Huntington, who created nearby Brookgreen Gardens. The house is open for tours, and while the open central courtyard is inviting, the house itself has small rooms, concrete walls, and tiny, barred windows that are more reminiscent of a county jail than the beach home of one of America's richest and most influential families. Still, it is interesting, and it makes you even happier to get back into the sunlight for a long walk in the fresh sea air of the beach.

And what a beach! Three miles of completely pristine Atlantic oceanfront with sand so fine it squeaks beneath your sandals. Here, black-headed Bonaparte's gulls float on the ocean breezes, pelicans glide in formation just above the waves, and sandpipers and ruddy turnstones skitter back and forth along the edge of the surf.

This beach was part of the lands purchased by Archer and Anna Huntington in 1930. They had originally planned nothing more than a large summer beach estate for themselves, but Anna, in particular, was captivated by the beauty and untapped potential of the land. She began to create Brookgreen Gardens, which opened in 1932. Anna planned a world where natural and man-made beauty would blend. Today, visitors can stroll along paths shaded by 250-year-old oaks past brilliant flower beds, wonderfully elaborate fountains, and more than five hundred of the finest examples of American sculpture on display anywhere in the world.

The works include the A. A. Weinman's powerful and massive *Riders of the Dawn* and Carl Milles' delightfully fanciful *Fountain of the Muses*. Anna's own renowned sculptures are here as well, including her ethereal *Diana of the Chase*, which stands above a lily pond in the center of the Diana Garden. Beyond the formal gardens, numerous trails lead through the estate's thousands of acres of salt marsh and woodlands, which are maintained as a nature reserve.

Just north of Brookgreen Gardens, the historic fishing community of Murrells Inlet sits at the edge of a spectacular salt marsh, which has navigable channels that lead out past the sandy end of Huntington Beach to the sea. The shrimp boats and commercial charter fishing boats attest to the inlet's reputation as South Carolina's seafood capital, but if you aren't convinced, then pulling your chair up to a table at any of the area's thirty or more renowned seafood restaurants should do the trick.

The history of Murrells Inlet is long and filled with legends of pirates, ghosts, and rebel blockade runners. One of the most popular watering holes in Murrells Inlet is called Drunken Jack's. Its name comes from nearby Drunken Jack Island, where, according to legend, an old pirate was accidentally left behind by his shipmates, along with many cases of rum. Several weeks passed before he and the rum were missed, and when the pirates returned, they found the island strewn with a wandering trail of empty bottles at the end of which were the bones of Drunken Jack.

A gifted and nationally recognized sculptor, Anna Hyatt Huntington was the creator of Brookgreen Gardens. In addition to creating the gardens and establishing arts programs, she and her philanthropist husband, Archer Huntington, donated their home and the adjoining coastal property, which became Huntington Beach State Park, to the state. Brookgreen Gardens

PART III

THE SANDHILLS AND COTTON COUTNRY

FACING PAGE:
A field of cotton reaches white fluffy maturity near Florence. The harvesting of this crop, which used to be painstakingly done by hand, is now completed in a few hours by a mechanical harvester that replaces five hundred pickers.

ABOVE:
A produce sign proclaims the bounty of summertime along a country road near Lake Murray.

ROUTE 8

Begin at the junction of Interstate 95 and South Carolina Highway 38. Follow Highway 38 north to Blenheim and turn right (east) on South Carolina Highway 381 toward Clio. Watch carefully for signs to Blenheim Mineral Springs, about 0.3 mile on the right. From Clio, turn left (west) onto South Carolina Highway 9 to Bennettsville. To visit the Jennings-Brown House and the Marlboro County Museum, stay on Business 9; from there, turn left on Main Street and left on South Marlboro Street. Then return to Main Street and head south. Continue on U.S. Highway 15 south to Society Hill and Hartsville. Then take the South Carolina Highway Business 151 exit and follow Fourth Street/Darlington Highway into town. Turn left on West Carolina Avenue to Kalmia Gardens. Continue on West Carolina Avenue a short distance and turn left (south) on Kellytown Road to the small town of Ashland. Turn south on Ashland Stokes Bridge Road to reach U.S. Highway 15 to Bishopville. In Bishopville, turn right on West Cedar Lane to reach the Cotton Museum. Return to U.S. 15, continue south a short distance, and turn right on Broad Acres Road to reach Pearl Fryar's Topiary Garden.

A few years back, say 20 million or so, the sandhills of South Carolina were *the* place to hang out at the beach. This was a happening place during the Miocene epoch. Today, to the east of the sandhills lies the state's vast, flat coastal plain, which was once the floor of that ancient sea. To the west is the fall line where the ancient sea ended and the land rose abruptly. The fall line runs hundreds of miles to the north and south, and several East Coast cities, including Washington, D.C.; Atlanta, Georgia; and South Carolina's Columbia were built along this line, which marks the farthest navigable point on the eastern rivers. The rapids created as rivers tumbled over the fall line made further upriver travel impossible.

Largely destroyed in the Civil War, Columbia is now a gracious and modern small southern city that boasts an exceptional university and a high quality of life. Elsewhere around the sandhills, small towns like McBee, Chesterfield, and Pageland maintain a laid-back pace of life, while the towns of Camden and Cheraw have retained much of their nineteenth-century charm.

No longer barren windswept dunes, the sandhills today are blanketed with deep green pine forest and are dotted with ponds and lakes. This wild (and wildlife-filled) region is one of the natural delights of South Carolina's largely undiscovered interior. In this relatively flat region, rivers flow slowly, and in the rainy season they spill past their banks, creating vast swamps of cypress and tupelo gum trees. The largest and best known of these is the Congaree Swamp, an extensive tract of bottom-land forest that is one of America's newest national parks. Filled with wildflowers, butterflies, and brilliantly colored birds, this watery wonderland offers up an unforgettable experience to hikers as well as those adventurous enough to explore it on guided kayak or canoe trips.

COTTON COUNTRY
BLENHEIM TO BISHOPVILLE

The story of America's feistiest ginger ale begins in 1783 with a life-or-death chase and a lost shoe. As the story goes, Tory troops were pursuing Patriot sympathizer James Spears through the woods near present-day Blenheim when his shoe stuck in the mud surrounding a waterhole. Being a man of keen judgment, he kept right on running, leaving his shoe behind.

In those days, shoes were valuable items, and when Spears (who had successfully eluded his pursuers) returned to retrieve his shoe, he also took time to take a drink from the natural spring and found the cool, mineral-rich water to be refreshing. Word of the spring's invigorating waters spread, and before long several planters located their summer homes nearby. In the late 1800s, Dr. C. R. May was treating patients with stomach problems and advised that they drink the spring waters. When they complained of the mineral taste, he added strong Jamaican ginger, and Blenheim Ginger Ale was born.

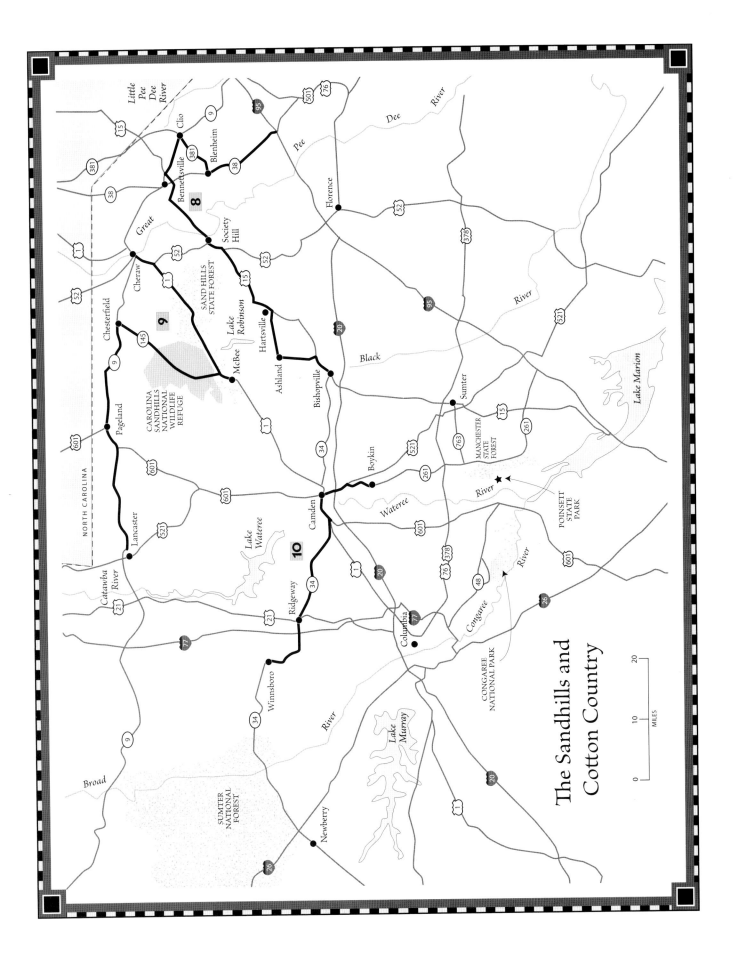

The Sandhills and Cotton Country

Cotton, once the economic engine of South Carolina, is becoming a popular crop once again. After the cotton flower drops off, a cotton "boll" begins to grow. When the boll matures, it bursts open revealing the white fluffy cotton inside.

Both horticultural and arts groups have praised the creative genius of Pearl Fryer's unique and fascinating topiary garden.

Pearl Fryar sits in his celebrated topiary garden in Bishopville. A mechanic and self-taught artist, he has garnered international acclaim with his amazing works of art.

May and a colleague began bottling and selling the drink in 1903. Hot, spicy, and totally unique, Blenheim was South Carolina's best kept secret until 1983, when the TV show *PM Magazine* did a segment on the soda. Later, Charles Kuralt featured the diminutive bottling company on his famous *On the Road* series, and the company has since been profiled in magazines such as *Playboy* and *Forbes*.

The original Blenheim Bottling Plant was renovated in 1983, but was quickly overwhelmed by growing demand. So the owners built a new bottling company nearby and plan to turn the old facility into a museum focused on the history of bottling. The old bottling plant is just a stone's throw from where the original mineral water bubbles out of an artesian spring near the side of the quiet country road. People still come from miles around to gather the water in plastic jugs to take home.

This region is the heart of South Carolina's cotton country, a world of timeless small towns and vast fields of cotton that few tourists get to see. "King Cotton" brought a great wave of wealth to this region in the late 1800s. That prosperity left behind a wonderfully preserved collection of mansions and historic commercial buildings in Clio (pronounced Cly-o), a small town that at one time claimed to have more millionaires per capita than anywhere else in America. In 1895, the train arrived to help town residents get their tons of cotton to market. The train tracks were dismantled in 1941, but the train station remains and now is a charming tourist bureau where you can pick up a map with a walking tour of the historic district. The town has a working cotton gin, and in the fall you can watch as machines separate the oily seeds from cotton fibers just as they have for over a hundred years.

From Clio to Bennettsville to Society Hill, two-lane country roads lead through long stretches of lovely agricultural lands to small towns with well-tended historic districts and lovely antebellum and Victorian homes. In Bennettsville, the elegant Jennings-Brown House (with period furnishings) stands next to the Marlboro County Historical Museum, which features an interesting collection of artifacts ranging from prehistoric native tools to a hollowed out gum-tree log that local resident Mason Lee used as a bed.

Born in 1770, Mason Lee was struck by lightning at an early age, which left him "different." Terrified of witches and demons, he slept in his log bed and lived a reclusive life, but still managed to amass a $50,000 fortune, which he left to the states of South Carolina and Tennessee. The will was contested in a famous legal case that is still studied in law schools today.

Hartsville is another pretty town that time seems to have passed by. It was founded by Thomas Hart, who was awarded 8,000 acres of land here in 1817. Today, Hart's original plantation is home to Kalmia Gardens. The gardens were planted in the 1930s by May Coker. When she took over the property, it had declined to little more than a dump site. Many locals thought "Miss May" was crazy when she announced her plan for fine gardens on the steeply sloped and heavily wooded site. But with boundless energy and good

KING COTTON

While rice brought unprecedented wealth to the Low Country, it was Eli Whitney's invention of the cotton gin that allowed cotton production to explode across South Carolina, bringing a second wave of prosperity that was unlike anything seen before.

Sea Island cotton had been grown as a secondary crop along the coast for years. It produced superb cloth, but remained a less profitable crop because picking seeds out of the cotton boll was difficult and time consuming. Sea Island cotton also could not be grown inland; while short-fiber "upland" varieties of cotton would grow on South Carolina's vast piedmont, their seeds were almost impossible to remove by hand.

Whitney's cotton gin changed all that. Ironically, Whitney saw little profit from his invention. Planters deemed his charge of 20 percent of the cotton crop so onerous that they began copying his technology and building their own "improved" gins. With gins available across the state, short-staple cotton became not just practical, but also very profitable, and farmers rushed to clear land and plant the white gold.

Cotton planting and harvesting was still labor intensive, and with the wild growth of cotton farming came a huge demand for slaves. The slave markets of Charleston and Savannah prospered as never before.

In the 1820s, cotton from Mississippi and Texas began flooding the market, triggering a series of boom-and-bust cycles, but cotton profits still vastly outweighed the losses. Throughout the first half of the 1800s, South Carolina was awash with money and speculative fever. Planters built ever-grander and more elaborate houses and entertained like royalty. The value of land skyrocketed. In all, the fortunes produced by King Cotton were some of the largest the young nation had ever seen.

The Civil War and the emancipation of the slaves created a dramatic decline in cotton production and prompted the rise of the sharecropper system. Landless farmers would contract with plantation owners, receiving the use of a small plot of land in return for helping to produce the plantation's large crop. But it was difficult for sharecroppers to get ahead, and in many ways sharecropping was little better than the slavery it replaced. Still, as more acreage went under the plow, post-war cotton production in South Carolina recovered and slowly grew.

The days of King Cotton came to an abrupt end with the boll weevil infestation of 1919, which destroyed over 70 percent of the state's crop. The state's boll weevil eradication program, begun in the 1930s, was followed by the development of pest-resistant strains of cotton. Today, cotton production is once again flourishing in South Carolina.

A print that appeared in Harper's Weekly *depicts a rather idyllic version of the cotton harvest in South Carolina in the late 1800s.* Library of Congress

An antique tractor is just one of the many old farm implements on display at Mac's Pride Antique Museum on the McLeod Farm in McBee.

At one time, more than 90 million acres of longleaf pine forest blanketed the southern United States. Today, less than 2 million acres remain, a large number of which are in the Carolina Sandhills National Wildlife Refuge. These woods are also home to the endangered red-cockaded woodpecker.

An imposing statue of famous orator, senator, and former U.S. vice president John C. Calhoun stands under the copper dome of the South Carolina State House in Columbia.

humor, "Miss May's Folly" began to take shape and thrive, even through the hardships of the Great Depression.

The name Kalmia comes from the Latin word for mountain laurel, which is found in profusion throughout the gardens. Also here are brilliant beds of flowers and vibrant green spaces made colorful and fragrant with the blooms of azaleas, camellias, tea olives, roses, and wisteria.

From Hartsville, it's just a short run south and west to Bishopville, where you'll find the thoroughly wonderful Cotton Museum. This small museum presents the story of King Cotton through excellent displays and a superb collection of nineteenth- and early-twentieth-century photographs and artifacts. To its credit, the museum doesn't shy away from portraying the hardships of slavery or the difficult years of post-Reconstruction share-cropping. There are also displays covering the cotton-mill era that was so important to South Carolina's economy in the early twentieth century.

A short distance outside of town, an unassuming residential area is home to Pearl Fryar's Topiary Garden. The garden got its start when Fryar was coming out of a nursery and spotted a small topiary. According to Fryar, the manager gave him a five-minute lesson in shearing a plant to a specific shape, and he went home to try the art on his own hedges and trees. What began as a curiosity quickly became a passion, and Fryer bought and planted more shrubs on which to practice.

Not content to create the typical topiary animal shapes, he painstakingly sheared and trained his plants into complex and beautiful shapes, and his topiaries quickly entered the realm of modern art.

As his garden grew to fill the three acres surrounding his home, news of his unique art began to spread. He has been interviewed by major gardening magazines and by Oprah Winfrey, as well as being featured on several cable television gardening shows. Today, visitors and collectors come from around the world to enjoy the one-of-a kind beauty found in Fryar's backyard.

African-American laborers load a wagon full of cotton crop around the turn of the twentieth century in South Carolina. Voyageur Press Archives

WATERMELONS, SANDHILLS, AND JAZZ
LANCASTER TO CHERAW

Nothing says summertime in the South like watermelon, and since 1940, the little country town of Pageland has billed itself as the "watermelon capital of the world." Although this slogan may be a bit of marketing, no one who lives here would deny that Pageland's sandy soil and long, warm summers seem to be a perfect match for growing big, sweet watermelons. Watermelon fever reaches a high point here in July during Pageland's Watermelon Festival. Begun in 1951, the weekend festival is a celebration of small-town America, complete with a parade, country music, a street dance, amusement rides, and plenty of ice-cold, ever-so-ripe, juice-running-down-your-chin watermelon.

If you don't happen to travel though Pageland on that particular July weekend, you can still find local watermelons here from late June through August at produce stands all along South Carolina Highway 9.

This is a quiet corner of South Carolina. From Pageland to Chesterfield, the highway passes through a pretty landscape of pine forest and small-scale farms, loosely following the route that General William Tecumseh Sherman rode as he swept across northern South Carolina before heading into North Carolina to join forces with the larger Union army.

From Chesterfield, South Carolina Highway 145 heads south through the heart of Carolina Sandhills National Wildlife Refuge. Before the arrival of Europeans, over ninety million acres of the southeastern United States were blanketed in a vast expanse of longleaf pine forest like that found here. This unique ecosystem depends on lightning strikes to light fires that sweep through huge sections of the forest every few years. The fast-moving fires are fueled by the dry pine needles and wiregrass that cover the forest floor. The forest's fire-resistant pine trees are largely undamaged by the blazes, but the fire suppresses hardwoods and other growth, leaving only the hardy wiregrass to recover the forest floor. What remains is mile after mile of open parklike forest. Today, only about two million acres of longleaf pine remain in the South, and much of it can be found in South Carolina.

The best place to start your visit to Carolina Sandhills National Wildlife Refuge is the visitor center just off U.S. Highway 1 north of McBee, where you can pick up information on hiking trails and fishing ponds (license required) and a map of the extensive network of roads open for mountain biking.

Just a few miles from the Sandhills visitor center is the small town of McBee (pronounced MACK-bee). The best time to visit this town is in late February or early March, when thousands of acres of peach orchards bloom, creating a soft pink haze that contrasts vividly against

ROUTE 9

From Lancaster, follow South Carolina Highway 9 east to Pageland and on to Chesterfield. In Chesterfield, turn south on South Carolina Highway 145 and drive through Carolina Sandhills National Wildlife Refuge to U.S. Highway 1. At that junction, turn south on U.S. 1 to McBee. From there, turn left (east) on South Carolina Highway 151 to McLeod Farms. Then return to McBee and head north on U.S. 1 to Cheraw.

The forests and unspoiled lakes of the sandhills are a sportsman's paradise. Here a fisherman wiles away a late afternoon casting for bass.

Pageland bills itself as the watermelon capital of the world, and watermelons are certainly a popular item at this roadside stand just outside the town.

Peach blossoms on the McLeod farm in McBee.

the emerald green hillsides. Walking through one of these pink orchard wonderlands as the sun's rays first strike these flowering branches is an otherworldly experience.

The next best time to visit McBee is in July, when the ripe, juicy peaches appear at the fruit stands. Just the rich, flowery smell of the sun-ripened peaches is a treat, but biting into that sweet, juicy goodness is as good as life gets.

You can have both of these experiences at McLeod Farms, just east of McBee. Surrounded by extensive peach orchards, the McLeod Farms Market also sells a wide range of other local produce, jams, jellies, and ice cream. Just across from the market, Mac's Pride Antique Museum contains a fascinating collection of antique tractors, farm machinery, cars, farm tools, furniture, and road signs collected by the McLeod family over many years.

The last stop on this route, Cheraw, is one of those great South Carolina towns that few visitors discover, but is bursting with character, great historic buildings, friendly residents, and charm. A lot of Cheraw's lure can be traced to the fact that General Sherman chose not to burn the town to the ground as he had so many others in the state—although his troops did accidentally set off a munitions explosion that leveled many of the commercial buildings in the downtown area. Most of the town's finer homes and businesses were spared, however, and today Cheraw boasts over fifty beautiful antebellum buildings in its historic district. The town also is home to scores of fine Victorian homes and buildings that date to around 1900, when cotton farming brought a second wave of prosperity to this corner of the state.

Cheraw's visitor center offers a brochure with a walking tour of the town's historic district; it includes descriptions of the most important buildings. At the top of the list is the old St. David's Church. Built in 1770, this was the last Anglican church built in the colonies under King George III. The interior of the central section of the church looks much as it did when the church was completed. During the Revolutionary War, the church was used as shelter by both British and Patriot troops. Likewise during the Civil War, both Union and Confederate armies used the church as a hospital. Other historic buildings in Cheraw include the 1925 Lyceum Museum and the lovely Greek Revival–style town hall built in 1858.

Cheraw, in South Carolina's inland sandhill region, is a town rich with gardens, parks, and architectural heritage, but is also known for its most famous native son—jazz legend Dizzy Gillespie. Born John Birks Gillespie on October 21, 1917, "John Birks" was already known to many of Cheraw's 3,500 locals by the time he was ten. He became so proficient at sneaking into the town movie house that the manager finally gave him the job of keeping other kids out, which allowed him to see all the movies for free. In fact, in his diary, he wrote that "mischief, money making, and music captured all my attention" while growing up in Cheraw.

Gillespie's father died when he was just ten, forcing the family to work hard to put food on the table. Because he had a near perfect sense of rhythm, Gillespie danced for money at the Chiquora Club in town as a boy. He learned music by ear and played the piano and the trombone before switching to the trumpet. His first paid musical gigs were at a "white" high school dance and Cheraw's town hall. Gillespie went on to college and followed his mother to Philadelphia, where he began a long career that included playing trumpet with some of the greatest Big Bands of the era. Nicknamed for his zany onstage antics, he earned his fame as a pioneer in bee-bop jazz and as a founder of Afro-Latin Jazz. He also inspired many modern jazz greats, including Miles Davis.

The site of his family home in Cheraw is now a park that features musical-themed metal benches and sculptures designed by local children under the direction of artist Bob Doster. Doster also created the park's aluminum fence, which depicts bars of music from one of Gillespie's best-known works, *Salt Peanuts*. The town's main square has a statue of Gillespie that depicts his signature puffed cheeks blowing into his trumpet.

Dizzy passed away in 1993, and although he never lived in Cheraw after his childhood, he returned often to visit friends. And he often started his concerts by saying, "I'm Dizzy Gillespie from Cheraw, South Carolina."

Born and raised in Cheraw, Dizzy Gillespie never forgot his roots and often returned to visit old friends. His hometown also never forgot him, as he was known for his music and mischievous ways, even as a boy. Library of Congress

Completely refurbished in 1996, the stage of the
Newberry Opera House is once again the site of
nationally acclaimed musical and stage
performances.

The miller watches over the old mill in historic
Boykin, where the water-driven grindstones
turn out grits and cornmeal just as they did one
hundred and fifty years ago.

One of many small, charming towns in the heartland of South Carolina, Ridgeway has the distinction of being home to the world's smallest police station.

Two rockers and an old barber's chair welcome customers who are waiting for car repairs at this old-time service station in Ridgeway.

ROUTE 10

From Winnsboro, follow South Carolina Highway 34 east to Ridgeway, and continue east on Highway 34 to U.S. Highway 1. Take U.S. 1 into Camden. After exploring Camden, head south on U.S. Highway 521 to Historic Camden Revolutionary War Site, and then continue south on U.S. 521 to the junction with South Carolina Highway 261. From there, take Highway 261 south to Boykin.

The distance from the world's smallest police station to where the last Union soldier fell in battle during the Civil War is just over twenty miles, but those twenty miles traverse almost three centuries of American history.

Visitors driving into Ridgeway for the first time may feel that they have slipped into a time warp. Within the town borders, it could easily be 1955 or even earlier. The town's water tower rises high above Rufus and Company Hardware Store, where you can still buy screws individually and nails by the pound. Down the street, the 1930s-era glass-topped pumps at the gas station still fuel cars, and customers waiting for their tires to be patched can take a seat in the rocking chair under the portico.

Ridgeway's biggest claim to fame is that it is home to the world's smallest police station. The station overlooks what was once a busy "cotton yard," where farmers brought their mule-drawn wagonloads of cotton to be ginned and sold. On their way out of town, they would water their mules at a fountain-fed trough. When the era of the mule had passed, the town leaders needed a shelter for their one-man police force, so they built a floor over the fountain and added four walls, creating a police station just large enough for the police officer, his desk, a small counter, and a chair for one complainant. The small station closed in 1990 and became the town's visitor center. The new police station, which may qualify as the world's second smallest police station, is right next door. Barely twice the size of the first station, it was originally built to house the town's single fire engine.

From Ridgeway, Highway 34 leads through a green patchwork landscape of farms and fields to Camden. Originally laid out in 1733, Camden was the first town to be settled in inland South Carolina. Quakers were among the earliest residents, and they were followed by large numbers of Scotch-Irish settlers. The town itself has undergone numerous changes over the years. Originally called Fredericksburg, it later became known as Pine Tree Hill. Finally, successful trader Joseph Kershaw arrived and convinced residents that Pine Tree Hill was a provincial name and they should rename the town Camden.

Although he was successful in that campaign, Kershaw demonstrated stunningly poor timing by building his exquisite new mansion in Camden on the eve of the American Revolution. General Charles Cornwallis had already arrived in the South, quickly conquered Charleston, and headed inland to set up command centers from which to quell the unrest. When Cornwallis arrived in Camden, he took one look at Kershaw's fine new house and decided it would become his new headquarters.

From Camden, the British routed the untrained Patriot militia, led by colonial General Horatio Gates, in one of the most disastrous Patriot defeats of the war. Many captured Patriot soldiers were hung as traitors in Kershaw's backyard. After that victory, however, the war went poorly for the Brits in this region.

Kershaw, who had been labeled dangerous by the British and banished to Bermuda, eventually returned and lived out his life in his beautiful house. During the Civil War, the house was burned to the ground, and with the passing years, the site became so overgrown and forgotten that it took an archaeological excavation to relocate the foundations. Two hundred years after its construction, the town fathers rebuilt the house in exact detail, and today it's the focal point of the Historic Camden Revolutionary War Site, a 107-acre site that includes the original town grid of Camden. Also here are reconstructions of the British military fortifications, the 1785 John Craven House, log cabins from the early 1800s, and the 1795 McCaa House.

One of the most interesting attractions in town is the Quaker cemetery. Although Quakers are renowned for being peace-loving people, this cemetery is the final resting place for many people who died fighting. Among the head-stones, you'll find the graves of Dr. Roger Clark Todd, a Confederate army doctor who was Abraham Lincoln's brother-in-law; Confederate spy Josephine Brown; Captain Benjamin Carter, one of seven Revolutionary War veterans buried here; and Colonel William Shannon, who lost the last duel fought in South Carolina. Also here is the tombstone for Agnes of Glasgow who, as leg-end says, followed her British soldier lover barefoot to the New World and died here without ever finding him. Many believe her ghost still wanders the streets of Camden after dark, seeking her lost love.

From Camden to Boykin, this route travels through some of the oldest productive farmland in South Carolina. These lands were settled by William Boykin in 1755, and the crossroads settlement of Boykin has been owned and run by the Boykin family throughout its history. William's son, Burwell Boykin, was a successful farmer who substantially expanded the family holdings, adding a large mill pond that powered a cotton gin, saw mill, and grist mill. The grist mill still operates on a varying schedule, and the miller demonstrates grinding corn into meal and grits. The grits are considered some of the best in the Carolinas, and they are packaged and sold in the mill, as well as in the nearby Boykin General Store.

One of the loveliest historic houses in Camden, Kamshcatka was built in 1854 and was the winter home of the William F. Buckley family for many years. Library of Congress

The town of Boykin has seen more than its share of history. On April 18, 1865, it was the site of the aptly named Battle of Boykin's Mill, in which a handful of local Confederate militia and home guard, mostly old men and boys, engaged a much larger force of Union troops (which included a large contingent of African-American troops from the company made famous in the movie *Glory*). The fight was short and intense, and the Confederates eventually retreated, having successfully halted the Union troops for a day. It was during this fight that a lieutenant of the 54th Massachusetts became the last Union officer to die fighting in the Civil War. Also noteworthy is that among the Confederate troops was a fifteen-year-old volunteer named Burwell Boykin, son of Confederate Colonel Alexander Hamilton Boykin.

THE SAVANNAH RIVER AND THE SOUTHEAST PIEDMONT

Horses graze placidly in a pasture in front of a rural church near Aiken. Scenes like this are common in the central farmlands of South Carolina.

A field of sunflowers basks in the summer sunlight near Barnwell.

This quiet corner of the state is bordered on one side by the broad, slow moving waters of the Savannah River. Two hundred years ago, the planters from the coast came to this region seeking a summer escape from the heat, humidity, and fevers of the Low Country. They flocked to towns like Walterboro and Aiken and built fine summer houses here. A second wave of settlement came in the late nineteenth century when wealthy northerners discovered Aiken's mild winters and brought their horses with them. Today, Aiken is the hub of South Carolina's horse country. The hilly countryside surrounding the town is dotted with an abundance of pretty horse farms, marked by elegant barns, stables, and miles of immaculately painted white fences.

Beyond Aiken, ever-changing rural landscapes lie in every direction. This was once cotton country and may be again, as cotton is making a comeback. The small cotton gin in the tiny crossroads town of Cope is very busy at harvest time, while the nearby charming town of Denmark is attracting growing numbers of visitors, largely due to the efforts of artist Jim Harrison, whose gallery here is a popular attraction. Throughout this region, the backroads are full of virtually undiscovered towns, like Barnwell, that are loaded with attractive historic buildings and that uniquely inviting Southern small-town charm.

MANSIONS, MURALS, AND GARDENS
WALTERBORO TO DENMARK TO EDISTO GARDENS

In 1784, a group of rice farmers—eager to escape the oppressive heat, mosquitoes, and disease that summer brought to the Low Country—began searching for a warm-weather retreat. They wanted someplace relatively close to home that offered a higher altitude, cool breezes, shade trees, and good water. Their search ended fifty miles north of Beaufort in a place they called Hickory Valley.

These early residents (who later renamed their town Walterboro) built their houses high on pilings to avoid the low-lying "evening vapors" they believed brought disease. They had the right idea, although it would be nearly a century before scientists proved that malaria was carried by mosquitoes that rarely fly more than a few feet above the ground. Today, several of these "high houses" can still be seen on a walking tour of the downtown area.

Tourism and modern development have largely bypassed Walterboro, whose main street looks much as it must have fifty years ago. After a stroll around town, you can cool down in Hiott's Pharmacy, where the ice cream parlor is right out of the 1950s. Pull up a stool by the long counter and order a double-scoop sundae or banana split drenched in chocolate syrup, piled high with whipped cream and topped with a cherry. Walterboro is also home to the South Carolina Artisans Center. Inside, this modest house-turned-gallery presents an impressive collection

ROUTE 11

Begin by exploring Walterboro, and then take South Carolina Highway 64 northwest to the intersection with South Carolina Highway 641 and veer left (west) to Rivers Bridge State Park. Continue on Highway 641 to U.S. Highway 321 and turn north to Denmark. From Denmark, take South Carolina Highway 70 northeast to South Carolina Highway 332 and go east into Cope.
To complete the route, return to Highway 70 and continue northeast to Edisto Memorial Gardens on the west side of Orangeburg.

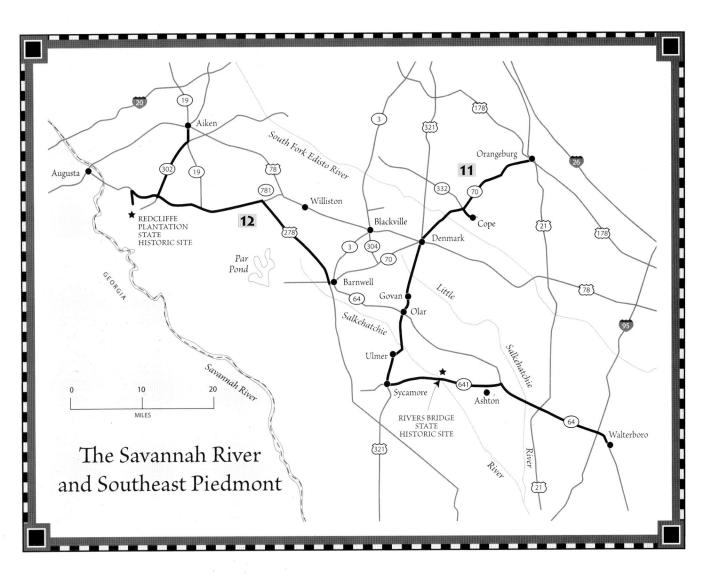

The Savannah River
and Southeast Piedmont

This Coca-Cola sign graces the Denmark gallery of artist Jim Harrison. A noted painter, Harrison started his career painting advertising murals like this one. Today, his paintings depict pastoral rural settings and often feature covered bridges, barns, and other buildings that have Coca-Cola and other advertising signs painted on them.

A roadside sign near Denmark advertises fresh corn and handmade canoe paddles.

An old farmhouse overlooks fields along a quiet rural road near Allendale.

The sky is reflected in the tranquil waters of this small lake in the Aiken State Natural Area.

of colorful and imaginative works created by some of South Carolina's finest artists. The shop's floor-to-ceiling shelves are crowded with an alluring array of pottery, glasswork, sculpture, jewelry, furniture, paintings, and more.

You could walk around all of downtown Denmark in five minutes, so it's hard to miss Jim Harrison's gallery. It's the beautifully refurbished turn-of-the-twentieth-century brick shop with a new Coca-Cola mural painted on the side. Harrison learned to paint advertising signs in the days when murals promoting Bull Durham tobacco, Levi jeans, and Coca-Cola adorned buildings in every small Southern town. After an eleven-year stint as a high-school coach, he returned to art. In this second career, he is acclaimed for his fine-art paintings and prints, which depict tranquil rural scenes of barns, buildings, and bridges, often adorned with the same type of advertising signs he painted as a youth. His paintings and prints have become enormously popular, and collectors from all over the country now travel to Denmark to seek them out.

Today, you'll find a couple of excellent restaurants here as well as the Carolina Collection, a surprisingly large and high-quality antique and curio shop that fills what was once AT&T's three-story plant. It was from this building that the first transcontinental phone call was placed in 1915. Denmark's little movie theater has also been restored, and many of the traditional businesses (like the hardware store, the original dime store, and the excellent Mennonite bakery) are thriving.

Outside of Denmark, South Carolina Highway 70 winds northward, crossing the south fork of the Edisto River and passing well-tended farms before turning into the tiny little crossroads town of Cope. In 1933, after Franklin Delano Roosevelt stopped a devastating run on the banks by giving them a holiday, only those banks with cash could reopen. The little bank of Cope survived, but moved to Orangeburg to be closer to the region's business center. The existing bank building languished, and the roof eventually caved in, but enterprising residents have painted the building with a clever mural depicting 1930s-era customers waiting outside.

Miles to the north, on the outskirts of Orangeburg, the lovely, tranquil Edisto Memorial Gardens lie along the banks of the Edisto, the longest blackwater river in the world. The gardens honor a 1865 Civil War conflict. In February of that year, a small force of just six hundred Confederate soldiers launched an attempt to slow down Sherman's advancing force of six thousand Union troops at the Edisto River Bridge. They hastily dug rifle pits from which they fired on the Union troops. The Southerners were soon flanked and routed, but they had managed to slow Sherman's advance, buying precious time for residents who were attempting to secure their valuables and flee to safety.

The Edisto Memorial Gardens were the creation of horticulturist Andrew Dibble, who developed them between 1937 and 1964. Today, the gardens cover more than 175 acres and paths here lead through a large rose garden, a sensory garden, a butterfly garden, and Centennial Park with its ornate fountain. A 2,600-foot boardwalk leads through the darkly beautiful cypress and tupelo swamp that borders the river. From mid-March to mid-April, the garden is particularly dazzling as the azaleas come into bloom. The rose gardens are also stunning, flowering almost continuously from April through November. There are inviting garden benches among the roses that offer a place to enjoy the splendor and fragrance of the blooms, watch the river, and perhaps reflect on how much human history weaves through this place of nature and beauty.

A RAMBLE THROUGH HORSE COUNTRY
AIKEN TO REDCLIFFE PLANTATION TO BARNWELL

It's difficult not to fall in love with the romance of horses and horse racing in Aiken, South Carolina. Here, you can stand at the rail of a simple, one-mile dirt track at sunrise and watch jockeys putting sleek thoroughbreds through their training paces. Morning mist often hangs over the track and the pounding of hoofs can be felt through the ground, as steam rises from the horses' flared nostrils and the jockeys' soft voices encourage their mounts.

This elegant, historic town is all about horses. In fact, many of the town's side roads are unpaved, the packed sand providing the perfect surface for the horses' hooves. Along these roads and in the two-thousand-acre Hitchcock Woods, locals riding horses of every size and shape clip clop underneath green arches of shade created by moss-covered oaks.

This town was founded when Southern planters discovered it was a pleasant place to spend the summer, away from the heat of the Low Country. In the late 1800s, wealthy northerners arrived to take advantage of the mild winters, and they brought their love of horseracing with them. Today, one of the best places to learn about Aiken's long love affair with horses is the Thoroughbred Racing Hall of Fame, which occupies a century-old stable on the Iselin estate. Aiken has bred many champions, including winners of the Kentucky Derby and Preakness Stakes, and their history is related here through artifacts, displays, and exhibits.

The fourteen-acre Iselin estate is now known as Hopeland Gardens. Like the museum, admission to the gardens is free. Inside the brick walls that surround the gardens, paths lead through an attractive collection of azaleas, camellias, and other flowering beds. Where the Iselin house once stood is a freeform goldfish pond, rimmed with ornamental plants and an observation deck.

A few miles southwest of Aiken, Redcliffe Plantation sits on a bluff above the Savannah River. The grounds of this elegant house are dotted with stately trees, some of which were planted by the original owner, James Henry Hammond. Hammond was a complex man and an avid horticulturist. He built Redcliffe as an experimental farm, a place of beauty where his discoveries could help a lot of South Carolina's farmers. His professional career included terms in the U.S. House and Senate, and he was also governor of South

ROUTE 12

Explore the town of Aiken, then drive south on South Carolina Highway 302 to U.S. Highway 278 and head west. From U.S. 278, turn south (left) onto Hammond Road. Then turn right onto Redcliffe Road to Redcliffe Plantation. To complete the route, return to U.S. 278 and head east to Barnwell.

An owner takes his horse on an early morning training run along the dirt roads of Aiken's horse district.

A pastoral scene in the horse country surrounding Aiken.

The street sign at the corner of Whiskey Road and Easy Street reflect Aiken's rough-and-tumble early days. Today, Aiken is a gracious town known for interesting shops, good restaurants, and a passion for all things horse.

Two trainers take their mounts out for an early morning run on Aiken's one-mile track.

A U.S. senator and governor of South Carolina from 1844 to 1846, William Aiken was also a successful rice planter and businessman. He and his wife extensively renovated the Aiken-Rhett house in Charleston and entertained lavishly there until the Civil War. Unfortunately, he never had the opportunity to visit the South Carolina town named after him.
Library of Congress

Carolina. A gifted orator, he coined the term "cotton is king" in a speech before the Senate.

However, he was also—even according to his friends—a braggart and a rampant womanizer. An avid secessionist, Hammond died a broken man in the closing days of the Civil War. His son Harry—by most accounts a stable, kind, and generous person—took it upon himself to live in and preserve his father's fine estate. After Harry's death, the estate fell into disrepair, but it was rescued in the 1930s by James Henry Hammond's great-great-grandson, John Shaw Billings, then editor of *Time* and *Life* magazines, who began restoring the old house. Today, the house and grounds are operated as a state park and are open for tours.

From Redcliffe, U.S. Highway 278 leads through mixed farmland before entering a vast pine forest that was once, but is no longer, part of Sumter National Forest. Why, you might ask, is it no longer a part of Sumter Forest? The answer to that question has a lot to do with the answer to another question: Where, in all of America, are atom bombs made? And the answer to that particular question is: Very, very near here. Or, at least they used to be.

The road you are traveling on goes through one of the world's largest top-secret nuclear weapons development sites. From the 1950s until the end of the Cold War, the Savannah River Site processed and refined nuclear materials for use in advanced weapon systems. Today, the site is largely involved in nuclear cleanup, but in an encouraging example of "swords to plowshares," a new 60,000-square-foot ultra-high-tech facility has been built here for research and development of new hydrogen fuel cell technologies that may someday help reduce global warming. Among the partners are the U.S. Department of Energy, several universities, and Toyota.

When General Sherman's troops rode into Barnwell, they burned many buildings, including the county courthouse, but they left standing the town's most unusual attraction: a vertical sundial. The sundial was made in Charleston in 1828 and given to the town by wealthy resident Captain Joseph Allen. Locals swear that this rare timepiece is accurate to standard time within two minutes. The lovely courthouse was rebuilt in 1878, and much of the downtown area is a pleasure to explore on foot. One of the buildings you will come across is the Church of Holy Apostles and Rectory. This charming cypress church with hand-carved pine benches was built in 1856 or 1857. Legend has it that before the Union troops entered the town, citizens removed and hid the stained glass windows, replacing them only after the invaders left.

Barnwell is also the birthplace of rock legend James Brown. In his autobiography, he paints an unglamorous portrait of growing up in a shack at the edge of town without electricity or running water. This portrayal, combined with his notorious bad-boy reputation, is probably the reason you'll not find a single monument or mention of him in the town today.

In 1998, a group of archaeologists and students under the direction of Dr. Albert Goodyear were digging at a site just south of the Savannah River Project, about ten miles outside Allendale, when they made a startling discovery.

Conventional archaeological theories maintain that the first humans arrived in North America by crossing the Bering Strait about thirteen thousand years ago. These people migrated slowly across the continent, arriving on the East Coast around twelve thousand years ago. However, at this site, workers discovered manmade tools at a level far deeper than anything found before. These tools were estimated to be at least sixteen thousand years old, dramatically challenging conventional scientific ideas.

But the discovery soon became even more interesting; additional excavations yielded more tools in even deeper levels, and in 2004, samples of vegetation from the deepest discovery levels were sent for carbon dating. Expecting a date of perhaps twenty thousand years old, Goodyear was astounded when the carbon dating showed that the level where the oldest tools were found was around fifty thousand years old.

Although other sites around the Americas have begun to yield samples that are older than the conventional scientific theory purports, the artifacts from the Allendale site, now called Topper, are by far the oldest evidence of humans in the New World. If supported, this discovery will dramatically alter our understanding of when the first humans really arrived in North America. Not surprisingly, this discovery has been challenged by numerous scientists, and it will, without a doubt, create a lively debate among scholars for years to come.

LAKE COUNTRY:
THE SOUTHWEST PIEDMONT

A single brightly colored balloon drifts above the lakes and woods near Anderson during the annual Anderson Balloon Festival.

Blackberries begin to ripen at Callahan's Fruit Stand near Belton.

If you ask residents or visitors in this area what they doing on the weekend, they are likely to say "Going to the lake, of course" and look at you as if they can't imagine why anyone would ask such a dimwitted question. From the 1940s through the 1970s, South Carolina built dams on an unprecedented scale, creating numerous sparkling blue lakes throughout the piedmont and foothills regions. These lakes are a big part of summertime fun in this region, and on warm weekends everyone who is anyone is heading to his or her favorite lake for boating, swimming, and fishing, as well as camping and picnicking in the many state and county parks that grace the lake shores.

Three of the largest lakes were created when huge dams were built along the upstream waters of the Savannah River. Covering 71,100 acres, Strom Thurmond Lake is the largest of the lakes, followed by Lake Hartwell (55,900 acres) and Richard B. Russell Lake (26,650 acres). Richard B. Russell Lake (named for a popular Georgia governor) is especially popular with nature lovers as development has been largely banned around its shore, leaving the lake pristine, tree-lined, and beautiful.

This portion of the state is also home to beautiful historic towns like Abbeville and Edgefield. Both of these towns played a significant role in the Civil War, and both have a wealth of exceptional antebellum homes and buildings in their downtown areas.

Near the foothills at the western end of this area is Clemson, a lively college town, where you can enjoy excellent restaurants, stroll through the green and floral grandeur of Clemson Botanical Gardens, and tour several of South Carolina's most fascinating historic homes. And throughout this region, inviting two-lane roads lead to new destinations, passing through fertile farmlands, small towns, and the deep pine woods of Sumter National Forest.

THE SEEDS OF HISTORY
ABBEVILLE TO THE GARDENS OF PARK SEED COMPANY AND NINETY SIX NATIONAL HISTORIC SITE

In 1908, an enterprising soul in Abbeville put together several facts and came to a brilliant conclusion. The first was that traveling Broadway and vaudeville shows put together in New York City and sent out by train to play in cities throughout the country were becoming very popular, and one of the most successful traveling show routes was from New York to Atlanta. The second fact was that Abbeville had a train station along that route and a good hotel. Lastly, Abbeville was the only town for miles around where thirsty actors and theater-goers could legally get a drink in mostly "dry" central South Carolina. All that was lacking to bring the traveling shows to Abbeville was a performance hall. That problem was solved by building one of the largest and prettiest opera houses in the South.

The theater's amazing 7,500-square-foot stage has now seen more than its share of famous performers. Actress Sarah Bernhardt played here, as did

ROUTE 13

From Abbeville, take South Carolina Highway 72 east toward Greenwood, and turn north onto Mill Road North (also called SC-S-1-61 or Klugh Road) just before Hunter's Creek Boulevard. Turn right on Old Hodges Road/Blue Jay Road and drive northeast to South Carolina Highway 185 and turn east at the junction. In the town of Hodges, take South Carolina State Highway 246 east to South Carolina State Highway 254 and turn south to the gardens of Park Seed Company. After visiting the gardens, return to Highway 254 and continue east and then south to South Carolina Highway 34. At the junction with Highway 34, continue south on South Carolina State Highway 248 to Ninety Six National Historic Site.

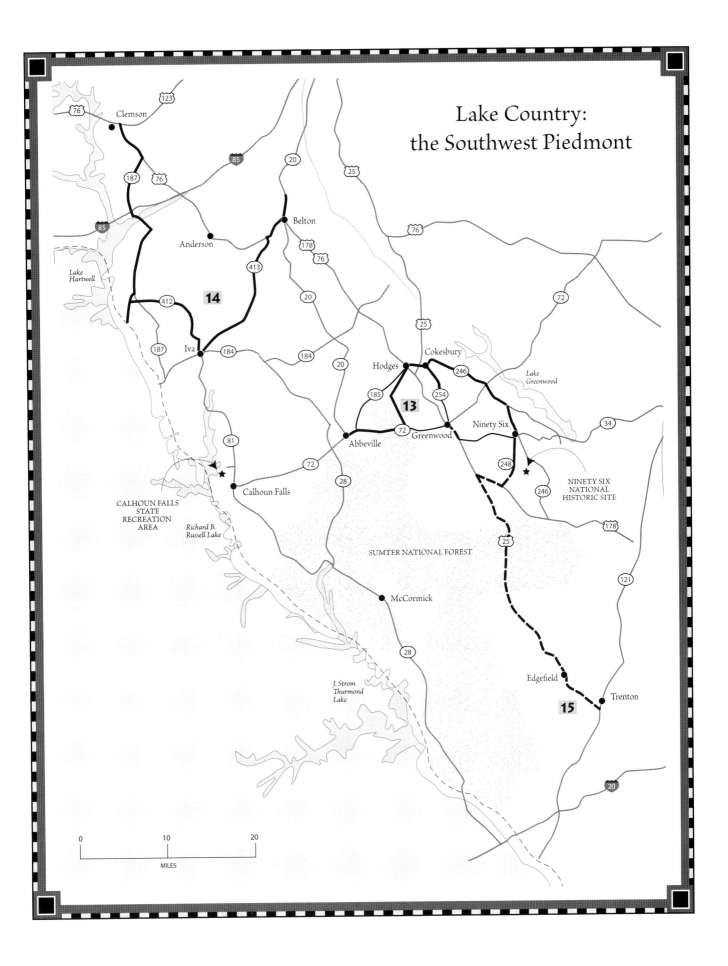

Lake Country:
the Southwest Piedmont

The pretty town square in Abbeville with its cast-iron town clock and brick town hall.

Price's Antique Shop, near Abbeville, recreates a 1930s-era rural gas station. Inside, visitors will find a wonderland of historic roadside advertising signs and automotive-related collectibles.

Crepe myrtle trees border a pastoral country road near Hodges.

A lone cannon overlooks the field where Patriot troops under General Nathaniel Greene made a determined attempt to overtake a star-shaped earthen fortress manned by 550 Loyalist troops in 1781.

The lovely demonstration gardens at the Park Seed Company attract thousands of visitors every year.

Fanny Brice, Groucho Marx, and Jimmy Durante. Real operas were staged here, too, as well as famous shows like *Fagg's Famous Lady Minstrels* and the *Ziegfield Follies*. Silent movies were shown starting around 1910, and later *The Jazz Singer* brought the first "talkies" to town.

Like many small-town performance halls, the theater fell on hard times in the 1950s and eventually closed. In the late 1960s, however, Abbeville began to undergo a renaissance, as newcomers discovered its charms and moved here. In 1968, the opera house was renovated and reopened to critical acclaim. In all, Abbeville's downtown is a far cry from the rugged frontier town that was first founded, at least in part, by Patrick Calhoun, father of legendary Southern orator and U.S. senator John C. Calhoun. The famous John C. also called Abbeville home for a while and had his law offices on the town square. Other notable residents have included Revolutionary War hero Andrew Pickens (who married Patrick Calhoun's sister, Rebecca) and famous American architect John Mills, designer of the Washington Monument.

From Abbeville to the town of Greenwood, Highway 72 crosses through a lovely rural section of South Carolina, where the gentle farmland is indeed emerald green in places. Just beyond Abbeville, watch closely on the right, and you'll spot what looks like a 1930s-era Texaco gas station complete with the glass-topped gas pumps. This unique creation is Price's Antiques, which specializes in automotive-themed antiques, including roadside signs, gas pumps, and automobiles. The shop is a treat to stroll through, and if you ask nicely, owner Alan Price might show you his pride and joy: a flawless, bright orange 1930 Chevrolet tow truck.

A few miles east of Price's, a turn north leads along narrow country lanes that pass small farms and the well-tended hunting retreats of country gentlemen. Blue Jay Road is particularly lovely with borders of azaleas and crepe myrtles that contrast beautifully with the rich green meadows and weathered wood fences. Just past the sleepy town of Hodges, turn south on Highway 254. You can't miss Park Seed Company, which is surrounded by acres of brilliantly blooming demonstration gardens that showcase some of the company's most popular varieties of flowers and decorative plants. Even if you have never bought anything from Park Seeds, the name may sound familiar to you. The reason is simple: Park has been selling seeds since 1868, and today it is the largest mail-order seed company in the world.

The company actually started in Libonia, Pennsylvania. At age sixteen, George Park had a strong interest in growing flowers, so he bought a hand printing press and printed a list of the seeds he had for sale. He took out an ad in the *Rural American* and quickly turned his $3.50 investment into $6.50. Shortly thereafter, he published the first Park Seed catalog. When he added articles and advice on gardening, his catalog distribution sky-rocketed, and by 1918 he was sending them to more than eight hundred thousand customers.

Late in his life, he married the young Mary Barratt and moved the seed company, first to Florida and then to Mary's hometown of Greenwood.

Gold and the Death of the Confederacy

On April 16, 1865, a travel-worn group of Confederate troops arrived in Abbeville, escorting an elegantly dressed woman. The woman was warmly greeted by wealthy resident Armistead Burt, who offered the lady rooms in his well-appointed house. She warned him that she was a wanted woman and was being pursued by Union troops, who might put his fine home to the torch for sheltering her. At this, Burt declared "Madam, I know of no finer use my house could be put to than to be burned for such a cause!"

The woman was Verina Davis, wife of Confederate president Jefferson Davis, and the troops were guarding not only her and her children, but also several heavy chests that contained the last gold in the Confederate treasury.

Abbeville has often been called the birthplace and deathbed of the Confederacy. The birthplace claim may be a bit overstated, although Abbeville did vote overwhelmingly to support South Carolina's Declaration of Secession on November 22, 1860, making it one of the first towns in the state to do so. But Abbeville has a much better claim to being the place the Confederacy died.

Verina, having no idea about the whereabouts of her husband, departed Abbeville, heading south to Georgia. A few days later, Jefferson Davis himself, along with a contingent of troops and officers, arrived in Abbeville, and Burt once again generously offered his home. Davis knew that the Union army was hot on his heels and his stay would have to be brief. He still held hopes that if he could reach his armies in Georgia, the Confederate cause could continue, but at four o'clock one afternoon, in the parlor of Burt's house, his officers dashed those hopes. They offered to use their troops to ensure his safety, but refused "to fire one more shot to prolong the war."

Davis left Abbeville a defeated man on the run, and he was captured by the Union army in Georgia a few days later. The Confederate gold was never recovered, and its fate has never been known.

Jefferson Davis, the president of the Confederate States of America and his wife, Verina. During the closing days of the Civil War, they lived a life of high adventure as they fled the advancing Union Army. Davis was eventually jailed for two years and stripped of his citizenship. After Davis' death, Verina moved to New York City and became an author. Library of Congress

The evening sunset spills across Lake Hartwell as a fisherman tests his luck against the lake's bass and bream.

It's not hard to find fans of the Clemson Tigers football team in southwestern South Carolina, as evidenced by this tiger paw symbol on a barn near McCormick.

A mustard field proclaims the abundance of South Carolina's farmlands.

Two youngsters enjoy the rocking chairs and homemade blackberry ice cream at Callaham's Fruit Stand.

Today, visitors come from all over the nation to tour the lovely gardens here. Tours of the greenhouses are available, and the gift shop offers a wealth of items related to gardens and gardening. The benches in the garden are good places to sit and watch a sunny day pass and think about what grew from a handful of seeds and a small printing press.

Ten miles east of Greenwood is the Ninety Six National Historic Site. This crossroads trading post was named by traders in the 1700s who mistakenly believed the town was located ninety-six miles south of the Cherokee town of Keowee. If you park your car and follow the mile-long winding footpath at the historic site, you arrive at a large, open green space, that looks tranquil and parklike. But climb the observation tower and the small hills and valleys that crisscross the field tell a different story. The foundations of a star-shaped fortress can be seen at the far end of the field. Here in 1781, General Nathaniel Greene and a thousand Patriot troops made a desperate attempt to seize the fortress held by 550 Loyalist troops under Lieutenant Colonel John Cruger.

A path leads past the battlefield to where the stockaded little town of Ninety Six once stood. At the time of Greene's attack, there were half a dozen buildings here, including a two-story brick jail. However, in July of that year, the Loyalists destroyed the town before they abandoned the area.

ROAMING AROUND LAKE COUNTRY
CLEMSON TO LAKE HARTWELL TO BELTON TO CALLAHAM ORCHARD

In downtown Clemson, you can't miss the big orange footprints—well, paw prints—running down the middle of the road. There is, in fact, a lot of orange everywhere you look—on flags and bumper stickers, on buildings and garden walls, and on barns all throughout this region. If you haven't caught on yet, Clemson is the home of the Clemson Tigers, and they are not just another college football team here. Tiger fans follow the team's ups and downs with a passion that borders on lunacy.

Paw prints aside, Clemson is a college town loaded with charm and all of the benefits of a bustling community, including good restaurants, great coffee shops, and a dandy garden with a big red caboose in it (more on that later).

Although he wasn't aware of it during his lifetime, John C. Calhoun is largely responsible for the founding of Clemson University. After the famous statesman's death in 1850, he left his plantation to his daughter and his son-in-law, Thomas Green Clemson. Clemson was passionately interested in agriculture and felt there was a need for agricultural research and education among South Carolina's farmers and planters. In his will, he left the land and the plantation house for the creation of an agricultural college. Over the years, the small college he sowed the seeds for grew into the highly regarded, multifaceted Clemson University. Today, Clemson regularly appears on lists of the best universities in the nation.

ROUTE 14

Begin in Clemson, and after exploring the town, go south on South Carolina Highway 28/ U.S. Highway 76. At the junction with South Carolina Highway 187, turn south on Highway 187 and continue past Interstate 85. When you come to a T junction, turn left, continuing southeast on Highway 187, which now becomes the Savannah River National Scenic Byway. Continue south on Highway 187 to the junction with U.S. Highway 29. Turn right on U.S. 29 and continue south to Lake Hartwell Dam Park, near the Georgia border. Then return north on U.S. 29 a short distance, and turn right (east) on South Carolina Highway 412 into Starr. Here you will turn right (south) on South Carolina Highway 81 to Iva. As you come into Iva, take a left on South Carolina Highway 184 and turn left (north) again on South Carolina Highway 413 to Belton. Highway 413 merges with U.S. Highway 76/178 near Belton. Stay on U.S. 76 into Belton and turn left (north) on South Carolina Highway 20. Take Highway 20 north to the intersection with Cheddar Road/Garren Road and turn right (east) to the Callaham Orchards fruit stand.

In the heart of the campus stands Fort Hill, Calhoun's beautifully preserved plantation home. The fine Greek Revival house stands on a manicured and landscaped lawn and is open for tours. It has not one but three white-columned façades, and when you tour the house, you will quickly find that its odd layout results from a hodgepodge assembly of attached rooms and additions. Calhoun and his wife had ten children over a period of eighteen years, and they kept the plantation carpenters busy adding rooms to the house to accommodate their growing family.

Another house worth visiting in Clemson is Hanover House. This small but elegant gable-roofed home was built in 1715, over sixty years before the Revolutionary War. For its builder, Huguenot planter Paul de St. Julien, Hanover House was both home and the place of business. It also had to serve as a frontier fortress, as the shuttered gun slots built into the thick basement walls attest.

St. Julien originally built his "big little house" overlooking the Cooper River. When the river was dammed in the 1930s, the house was in danger of being lost to the rising waters. Clemson University recognized the historic importance of the home and had it moved to its current site on the grounds of the Clemson Botanical Gardens, where students meticulously restored it to its original condition and opened it for tours.

Outside Hanover House, 295 acres of the Clemson Botanical Gardens are laced with inviting trails that lead past a butterfly garden, a children's garden, the horticultural gardens, the woodland wildflower garden, and a dozen more beautiful garden spaces. Many of the niche gardens here are sponsored by graduating classes, including the colorful caboose garden. Its

Fort Hill was the beloved home of John C. Calhoun. Today, it stands in the middle of Clemson University's campus, which was created on the lands of Calhoun's plantation. Pendleton District Commission

A "balloon glow" fills the evening sky during the annual balloon festival in Anderson.

South Carolina Highway 20 traces a lazy curve through lush meadows near Belton. South Carolina's piedmont is criss-crossed with lovely country roads like this one..

Boiled peanuts are a passion in many parts of South Carolina, but for those not raised on them, they are definitely an acquired taste.

Called the "cast-iron man" for his unbending views, John C. Calhoun was one of the most brilliant orators of the early nineteenth century. Along with famed senators Daniel Webster and Henry Clay, Calhoun formed a triumvirate known for fiercely debating the most critical issues of their era, bringing forth ideas and arguments that shaped the course of history.

Born into a Scotch-Irish planter family near Abbeville, young Calhoun was managing the family farm by the time he was fourteen. In 1802, he attended Yale University and eventually went on to study law. He returned to South Carolina to practice law and quickly rose in prominence. Elected to Congress in 1810, Calhoun became one of Henry Clay's "war hawks," who were prime instigators of the War of 1812. Calhoun served as vice president twice—once under John Quincy Adams and once under Andrew Jackson. However, he resigned during his second vice presidency to return to the Senate, where he felt he had more power.

Calhoun's speeches from the Senate floor were often impassioned and brilliantly argued. He was a staunch defender of the South's rights, which he astutely believed were often shortchanged by the more politically powerful North. He was also an unyielding advocate of slavery and state's rights, and he pushed for nullification rights (the ability for any state to declare a federal law unconstitutional if it felt the statute was not in the state's interest). This stance led to the nullification crisis of 1832, which came within a hairsbreadth of causing the breakup of the Union.

It was resolved by compromise, but Calhoun was convinced the die was cast. Shortly before his death, he wrote: "The Union is doomed to dissolution; there is no mistaking the signs. . . . I fix its probable occurrence within twelve years. . . . You and others of your age will probably live to see it; I shall not. The mode by which it will be is not so clear . . . but the probability is it will explode in a Presidential election."

In his final years, Calhoun retired a sad and defeated man to his beloved plantation of Fort Hill. He died in March of 1850, ten years before the election of Abraham Lincoln angered South Carolina and provided the impetus for the state to declare its secession from the Union.

A U. S. senator, two-term vice president, and renowned orator, John C. Calhoun was a passionate defender of state's rights. He longed for a workable union of the states, but accurately predicted that the Civil War would begin shortly after his death. Library of Congress

centerpiece is a big red caboose donated by Southern Railway. The caboose garden is a favorite meeting place for Clemsonites and marks the starting point for most of the garden's walking tours.

Beyond Clemson, a number of roads lead south and east through some of the state's most verdant and productive farmlands. This is also lake country, particularly along the Savannah River where three dams have created some of the largest manmade lakes in the South. The largest of these, with almost a thousand miles of shoreline, is Lake Hartwell.

The Savannah River National Scenic Byway follows the shore of the lake and occasionally crosses one of the myriad fingers of water that meander through the landscape. Here and there, views across the lake open up, offering a panorama of sapphire blue water against the deep green of the forested banks. On summer weekends, the water hums as hundreds of pleasure boaters, house boaters, and anglers head to their favorite coves.

Farther on, Highway 187 arcs to the west and heads for Georgia, passing below Hartwell Dam. The dam is huge; in addition to its 16,000 feet of earthen embankments, the concrete portion of the dam is 1,900 feet long and 204 feet high. It was poured with 880,000 cubic yards of concrete, which dam engineers once estimated could build a sidewalk from here to San Francisco.

If you want to spend a few minutes in a different state, continue past the dam and into Georgia for about a mile to the Hartwell Dam visitor center, where you can learn more about the history of the dam, its multiple uses, and the engineering feat required to construct it.

For the next twenty five miles or so, this route follows two-lane country roads that pass through the sleepy crossroads towns of Starr and Iva and then heads north through an ever-changing landscape of pretty farms, orchards, and woodlands. The quiet town of Belton is known for two things: its standpipe and its train station. The Belton standpipe, a castellated tower that rises 155 feet, is the town's water tower and official symbol. Built between 1908 and 1909, the tower is visible for miles around, and for many years, pilots flying over western South Carolina used the standpipe as a landmark. The town thinks so much of this unusual structure that it holds a standpipe festival each October that features a large antique car show and attracts up to ten thousand people a day.

Belton's second attraction, the beautiful train station, was built in 1853. Belton was originally created as a railway town, a stop on the Greenville and Columbia Railroad. Today, the station has been lovingly restored and houses the South Carolina Tennis Hall of Fame, which honors the many South Carolinians that have contributed to the success of local and state teams.

Beltonians, however, might choose Callaham Orchards, located just outside the town, as their favorite attraction. It seems a bit understated to call this a roadside stand, although in the open-air section it sells just-picked peaches, apples, nectarines, and other produce from the family's extensive orchards. But the real treat is inside, past the rows of homemade jams, jellies, and baked goods. Callaham's ice cream parlor boasts honest-to-goodness real ice cream, in a rainbow of delicious flavors, made fresh on the farm daily. The local favorite is the blackberry, made with berries that grow in the sunlit

The attractive town square in Edgefield is surrounded by turn-of-the-twentieth-century commercial buildings.

Garden decorations grace a yard near Sumter National Forest.

A truck is loaded with peaches for Cook's Roadside Market near Edgefield. The sun-ripened peaches are hand picked in orchards daily.

meadow right behind the building. Stand in line, buy at least a two-scoop cone, then step out onto the porch, where you can sit in a comfortable rocking chair and watch the afternoon sunlight wash across the rolling green fields. Lick, gaze, rock . . . and repeat.

SOUTH CAROLINA'S CRADLE OF SECESSION
NINETY SIX NATIONAL HISTORIC SITE TO EDGEFIELD AND TRENTON

ROUTE 15

As you leave Ninety Six National Historic Site, head south along South Carolina Highway 248 to the intersection with U.S. Highway 178. Head west on U.S. 178 for a short distance to the intersection with U.S. Highway 25. Turn south on U.S. 25 to Edgefield, and after exploring the town, continue on to the intersection with South Carolina Highway 121 near Trenton. Turn right at the intersection, continuing south on U.S. 25 through the Pecan allée.

You might not peg this quiet corner of the state as the birthplace of a giant in the civil rights movement, but here, a short distance from the hamlet of Mays Corner, was the home of Dr. Benjamin E. Mays. Minister, scholar, and educator, Mays was the man who Martin Luther King Jr. called "my spiritual mentor and intellectual father." Mays' house is long gone, but a roadside historic marker commemorates the site. It is just one of the many points of interest between Charleston and the Blue Ridge Mountains, along the South Carolina Heritage Corridor.

This route follows a section of the corridor from Ninety Six National Historic Site through the piedmont region's famous pastoral farmland and pine forest to Edgefield.

Maybe it's something in the water, but Edgefield has been the birthplace of more firebrand politicians than any other town in the state, and these politicians—good, bad, and indifferent—have contributed much to South Carolina's history. As a sign on the side of a downtown building boasts, Edgefield has been the home of ten of South Carolina's governors. The town was also the birthplace of Jim Bonham, hero of the Alamo, and it has been the home of several generals and U.S. senators.

Best known among these was Strom Thurmond, who at the age of one hundred became the oldest serving senator ever. He also served longer in the U.S. Senate (forty-eight years) than any other politician until 2006, when West Virginia Senator Harry Byrd served his forty-ninth year.

In Edgefield, where Thurmond returned after his retirement in January of 2003 and passed away shortly thereafter, he holds near godlike status. A statue of Thurmond looks out over the attractive green town square, which is surrounded with stately brick buildings that date to the 1800s. And there's a Strom Thurmond Memorabilia Room in nearby Magnolia Dale, an elegant historic town home, built in 1843 and now open for tours.

Blessed with extensive clay deposits, Edgefield became a center for pottery production in the early 1800s. Many of the early potters employed highly trained slaves to create simple but graceful pottery, including jugs, cups, bowls, and plates. Some of the most interesting of these (and the most sought after by collectors) are pieces made by a slave named Dave, who was not only a naturally skilled potter, but was also literate and trained as a typesetter. Other skilled slaves crafted face vessels, which were mugs, jugs, and other items that had distinctly African faces carved into them.

Today, just off the town square, you'll find Edgefield Potters, where artisan Steve Ferrell carefully creates stoneware based on designs that were made in Edgefield two hundred years ago. Ferrell has become renowned for the quality and authenticity of his simple, elegant jugs, face vessels, mugs, and other ceramic pieces. Visitors are welcome to stop in and chat with Ferrell as he crafts his wares, and perhaps take home a piece of South Carolina history.

Before you leave Edgefield, stop in at Ike's, a colorful roadside fruit stand near the town's visitor center. A passionate historian, woodcarver, and historical re-enactor, Ike can often be found at the stand, dressed in nineteenth-century farm clothes and carving historically accurate spoons, tools, and everyday utensils. With a little urging, he will spin fascinating and entertaining tales of Edgefield's colorful history.

A couple of miles beyond Edgefield, hunters and nonhunters alike will enjoy a stop at the National Wild Turkey Federation. This exceptional center is dedicated to teaching the public about the history of wild turkeys, and the federation's mission to restore and manage wild turkey habitat throughout America. The dioramas and exhibits are beautifully constructed, fascinating, and fun. The center puts on a presentation that begins with a full-sized animatronic old geezer, sitting on the porch of his shack, who alternately snoozes, snores, and wakes up to tell the story of how wild turkeys used to be plentiful in this area. Other displays describe the natural history of the turkeys and their traditional range, as well as the history of turkey hunting from prehistoric times to the early twentieth century (when devastating hunting practices were responsible for the near disappearance of this magnificent native American bird).

Just a few miles farther on Highway 25, you'll see Cook's Roadside Market on your right. This old-time family-owned stand offers a wide variety of fresh fruit and vegetables, most of which come from the family's own farm and orchards. Cook's is best known for its sweet, sun-ripened peaches, which are at their peak in the warm weeks of late June and July. Beyond Cook's, the highway turns to the right and goes through a long allée of stately pecan trees, and then passes through a stretch of picturesque farmland. Cotton fields flank the road, and you can see traditional cotton barns standing in the distance. Beyond them, orchards and fields stretch to the horizon.

PART VI

PEACH COUNTRY:
THE NORTHWEST PIEDMONT

FACING PAGE:
This elegant octagonal barn sits along a pretty country road near York.

ABOVE:
Baskets of ripe, juicy peaches await customers at the Sanders' family peach stand near Filbert. You can often find The New York Times *best-selling author Dori Sanders here, arranging peaches and chatting with customers.*

If you were to hover in a helicopter high above downtown York, you would see orchards stretching in every direction. This is South Carolina's Peach Country, and in June and July roadside stands are busy selling the best of the state's sun-ripened crop. Despite the fact that neighboring Georgia is thought of as "the peach state" (perhaps due to the peaches sported on Georgia license plates), South Carolina is actually the largest producer of peaches in the United States. Folks around here will be quick to tell you that the slightly cooler nights and sandy soil in this part of the state make for the very best tasting peaches.

This region also is home to some of the prettiest and most fertile agricultural land in the state. The rolling hills that lie between Charlotte, Chester, and Gaffney are a hundred vibrant shades of green and are filled with horse and dairy farms, peach and apple orchards, and fields bursting with corn, berries, wheat, cotton, and all manner of crops.

The land here was settled by Scotch-Irish in the mid-1700s, and they found it worth fighting for. This corner of the state saw more battles and skirmishes during the Revolutionary War than any other region in the South, culminating with the stunning Patriot victories at Cowpens and Kings Mountain. Also here is Brattonsville, which started as a pre-Revolutionary War era plantation and grew to be a thriving settlement.

RENAISSANCE, ROSES, AND REBELLION
CHESTER TO UNION TO SUMTER NATIONAL FOREST

ROUTE 16

From Chester, follow South Carolina Highway 9 northwest 30 miles to the junction with South Carolina Highway 49. Follow Highway 49 west 9 miles to Union. In Union, follow Highway 49 to South Carolina Highway 18 (Pinckney Street). From this intersection, turn left (south) and go two blocks. Next turn right onto Sardis Road. Follow Sardis Road south into Sumter National Forest to Rose Hill Plantation (also called Rose Hill State Park on some road signs).

The residents of Chester, South Carolina, are used to the occasional odd happening. It was, after all, in this quiet crossroads town that a finely dressed prisoner, being transported to Washington, D.C., in 1807, tore free from his armed guards, jumped up on a rock in the town center, and began to loudly berate his captors, claiming he was being framed and requesting civil authorities to intervene. This was no average prisoner, however. It was Aaron Burr, who served as vice president under Thomas Jefferson and killed Alexander Hamilton in an infamous duel.

Burr hated Jefferson and declined to run for a second term, instead traveling to the Southwest, where he launched a complex plot to convince the Southwestern states to secede, overthrow the government of Mexico by force, create a new country out of the two parts, and install himself as emperor. Upon being informed of the plot, Jefferson, who had no love for Burr, declared him to be a traitor and promptly had him arrested and hauled back to Washington for a trial.

In Chester, the populace mostly gaped at the spectacle, until one of Burr's guards pointed a pair of pistols at him and told him to get back on his horse. Burr angrily refused, and the guard, who wanted no part of shooting a man as important as Burr, threw down his pistols in frustration and grabbed Burr around the waist, bodily throwing him back on his horse.

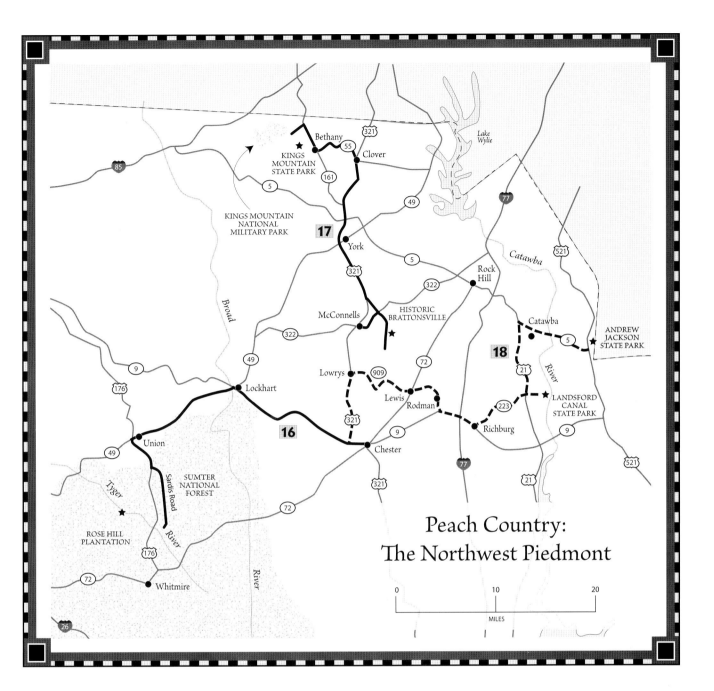

Peach Country:
The Northwest Piedmont

0   10   20

MILES

An old-time Coke sign decorates a building in downtown Chester. Many South Carolina towns are restoring or replacing these antique advertising signs that used to appear on buildings throughout the South.

An aging one-lane iron bridge spans a small stream on Sardis Road outside the town of Union.

A bloom-filled garden surrounds an outbuilding at Rose Hill Plantation in Sumter National Forest.

Built in 1832, Rose Hill Plantation served as the governor's mansion from 1858 to 1860 under Governor William Henry Gist. Often called the secession governor, Gist was instrumental in forging the path for South Carolina to secede from the Union.

Today, Chester is experiencing something of a renaissance. The attractive downtown streets are lined with mercantile buildings built in late nineteenth and early twentieth century, many of which sport colorful murals reflecting the town's two-hundred-year history.

Heading northwest out of Chester, South Carolina Highway 9 skirts the edge of Sumter National Forest and crosses the lovely Broad River to connect with South Carolina Highway 49. These rolling hills were once home to the Catawba Indians. In the 1700s and 1800s, the Catawba suffered decimating diseases, poverty, and persecution. In 1880, however, Mormon missionaries arrived and converted many of the Catawba, eventually leading some of them to a better life out West.

The first European settlers in this area were Scotch-Irish, who came south from New York and Pennsylvania along the Great Wagon Road in the 1750s. Hardworking, tough, and thrifty, they cleared land and established farms throughout the region. They were no lovers of England, though, and when the British army arrived to subdue the southern colonies in 1778, this region became a hotbed of resistance. A dozen or more major skirmishes occurred here that year, leading up to the stunning Patriot victory at Kings Mountain in 1780.

Heading south into Sumter National Forest, Sardis Road first travels through pretty, pastoral countryside, offering occasional hilltop views of the surrounding farmlands before entering green, heavily forested rolling woodlands. You have to watch closely for signs to Rose Hill Plantation State Historic Site, as the forest is so thick that the plantation is nearly impossible to see from the road.

Rose Hill played a pivotal role in the events that led to the Civil War. The estate was built in 1832 for William Gist, a lawyer and avid secessionist, who became South Carolina's governor in 1858. At the time, there was no governor's mansion in the state, so Rose Hill served as the center of government. Gist was one of many wealthy Southern planters who saw their way of life under threat. He campaigned tirelessly for separation of the Southern states—South Carolina in particular—from the Union. In fact, Gist sent his cousin—who had the improbable first name of States Rights—to speak for him in neighboring states and urge their secession from the Union.

The election of Abraham Lincoln as U.S. president in 1860 gave Gist's supporters all the impetus they needed. On December 20, 1860, a few days after Gist's administration ended, South Carolina seceded from the Union, catapulting the nation into the Civil War.

William Gist died in 1874 and was buried at Rose Hill. Then, like so many of the great Southern plantations, Rose Hill began a long slide into decay. By the 1940s, the house was so decrepit that it was considered for use as a target for bombers from Shaw Air Force Base. Fortunately, the plan was thwarted by local preservationists, who began the slow process of restoration.

Today, the state historic site is a tranquil and inviting place with lovely gardens filled with blooming roses and hummingbirds that flit busily from blossom to blossom. The house is open for tours and has been filled with period antiques, many of which belonged to the Gist family. So William might feel right at home if he were to return to his lovely plantation by the Tyger River.

PEACHES AND PATRIOTS
BRATTONSVILLE TO KINGS MOUNTAIN

Most visitors only see this quiet corner of South Carolina from the windows of their cars as they hurtle along Interstate 77. It's a shame, because this little-traveled region offers an inviting maze of country roads that meander through some of the prettiest agricultural land in the South. The orchards here produce bountiful harvests of gloriously large, sweet peaches, and locals are always quick to inform visitors that South Carolina is the largest peach producing state in the nation—not that other peach-proud state to the south!

And though it may not look it, this gentle region was once a hotbed of insurrection. In 1780, British General Charles Cornwallis arrived to "subdue the southern colonies." However, no one had bothered to tell the local farmers and frontiersmen that they were supposed to be subdued. Many were first- and second-generation Scotch-Irish who left their homelands with no love of the British, and they were dismayed to have traveled thousands of miles only to find redcoats at their door once again. Passionate followers of a Presbyterian faith that championed individualism and freedom and hardened by frontier life, they were a poor choice for the British suppression attempts. That year, in fact, George Washington wrote from his camp at Valley Forge that "if defeated everywhere else, I will make my last stand for liberty among the Scotch-Irish . . ."

By August of that year, it seemed as if Washington had been speaking prophetically. Having met virtually no resistance as troops swept through Georgia and much of South Carolina, the British arrived in South Carolina's northern frontier and conducted searches, looking for leaders of the local militia and other "rebels."

They proceeded to the South Carolina home of Colonel William Bratton, who was known to be an officer serving under General Thomas Sumter. Unknown to the British, Colonel Bratton had gathered a large Patriot force and was moving into the area. Legend has it that as the British set up camp at a farm near Bratton's home, his wife sent a trusted slave named Watt to locate her husband and his troops and inform them of the British position and strength.

The Patriots attacked at dawn, just as the British were climbing out of their tents. Caught by surprise, Captain Christian Huck leapt on his horse and tried to rally his men, but was shot and fatally wounded. The British attempted to flee, but ran into Patriot forces who blocked their escape and were forced to surrender. Although the Battle of Huck's Defeat was a relatively small skirmish, it provided the Patriots with a much-needed morale boost, and it was the precursor to the large and important Patriot victories at Kings Mountain and Cowpens.

ROUTE 17

Begin in McConnells at the junction of U.S. Highway 321 and South Carolina Highway 322. Follow Highway 322 east to Brattonsville Road. Turn south and continue on Brattonsville Road until you see signs for Historic Brattonsville. After visiting the village, return to Brattonsville Road and head north. Continue north on U.S. 321 when it intersects with Brattonsville Road. Follow U.S. 321 about 20 miles to the junction of South Carolina Highway 55 and turn left. Follow Highway 55 for about 6 miles to the junction of South Carolina Highway 161 and turn right. After about 3 miles, turn left on Park Road to Kings Mountain National Military Park.

Brattonsville's Homestead House was built in 1823 and it represents the growing needs of the expanding and prospering Bratton family. The house was used as a set for the Mel Gibson hit movie The Patriot.

The main room of the Colonel William Bratton House. It has been decorated to reflect its use as a country tavern in the Revolutionary War era.

One of the best preserved multi-era settlements in America, the houses and outbuildings at Brattonsville reflect periods from the 1770s to the late 1800s.

Re-enactors portray a Confederate artillery group loading and firing a field cannon at Brattonsville.

An example of pioneer strength and the American entrepreneurial spirit, this small family cabin, built by Colonel William Bratton before the Revolutionary War, served as a tavern and later as a school for young women. Culture and Heritage Museum Collection

William Bratton was not only a Patriot fighter. He was also an entrepreneur. Through his life and the following generation, his crossroads farm grew to include a tavern, a school for young ladies, a store, a post office, a blacksmith shop, and other profitable businesses. Eventually, this community became known as Brattonsville.

Today, with virtually all of the original buildings still standing, and many fully restored, Brattonsville uniquely illustrates the economic growth of a Southern rural community from the frontier era through the prosperity of the mid-1800s and the challenges of the post–Civil War years. If these buildings look strangely familiar, it may be because several of them served as sets in Mel Gibson's Revolutionary War hit movie *The Patriot*.

Like many of South Carolina's towns, York, on U.S. Highway 321 north of Brattonville, has a charming downtown. Its main street is lined on both sides with glass-fronted brick buildings from the late nineteenth and early twentieth century, many of which have been converted into antique shops and locally owned boutiques. The place for lunch here is the Garden Café, which serves ultrafresh ingredients in creative, delicious dishes that are a pleasant diversion from the chain restaurants and meat-and-two stops that are the mainstay in this corner of the state.

This is peach country, and the gently rolling farmlands north of York are blanketed with tidy peach orchards. In early spring, these fields are a visual tapestry of rich greens and cotton-candy pink as the trees come into bloom. If, however, you happen to travel this route between mid-July and mid-September (and you prove your brilliance by doing so), the region's country roads are dotted with peach stands selling South Carolina's tastiest export.

On U.S. 321 near Filbert, you'll spot Sanders Peach Stand on the left. You are here for two reasons. The first is to sample the peaches that are lovingly grown by the Sanders family and carefully placed in peck baskets to warm in the South Carolina sun. The second is to meet local legend and *New York Times* best-selling author Dori Sanders.

When she is not dashing around the country participating in writers' conferences or giving readings to promote her latest book, Sanders can be found here helping her brothers market the peaches that have been her life. Her best-known book, *Clover*, tells the story of an African-American girl raised by her white stepmother in rural South Carolina in the mid–twentieth century. Never one to be idle, Sanders spends a lot of her free time bustling around the stand, swiftly placing the ripest peaches on top of the baskets while simultaneously sharing her insights on life with customers.

The perfect experience here is to get Sanders to select one of her sweetest peaches and cut you a slice, the golden juice running like liquid sunshine, and then to sit and listen to some of her stories.

Heading north from the peach stand, it is just a short drive through pretty rural countryside to Kings Mountain, one of the least-visited but most fascinating national historic sites in the country. It was here in 1780 that the relentless juggernaut of the British army was brought to a sudden standstill by a ragtag army of "Overmountain Men."

Today, the best way to experience this site is to walk the mile-and-a-half trail that leads around the battlefield. Along the way, you'll pass the grave of Major Patrick Ferguson, who led the British troops. Legend has it that when he realized defeat was imminent, he drew his sword and rode headlong at the Patriots in a futile charge, falling after being shot as many as eight times.

Also of interest is the beautifully reconstructed farmstead at the adjacent Kings Mountain State Park. Built by the Civilian Conservation Corps in the 1930s, the log and stone buildings, farmhouses, and barns sit among pastoral fields defined by split-rail fences. It is easy to find yourself alone here, where the grass blows lazily in the breeze and birdsong fills the air. These quiet fields and sturdy buildings stand in silent testimony to the lives and spirit of three centuries of South Carolinians who lived and worked on this land.

ALONG THE CATAWBA RIVER
CHESTER TO ANDREW JACKSON STATE PARK

The roads leading north and east from Chester pass through gently undulating farmland that is some of the most fertile ground in the country. It's little wonder that the first waves of Scotch-Irish settlers, who arrived here in the 1750s, were prepared to undertake backbreaking labor to clear the land and risk their lives, first fighting Native Americans and later the seemingly overwhelming force of the British army, in order to maintain their hold on the land.

Through much of the 1800s, this was cotton country, and in every direction the fields stretched to the horizon. Then came the devastating boll weevil infestation of the 1920s that destroyed the cotton industry in South Carolina. Eventually, the region bounced back, and today the rolling fields support an incredible diversity of agriculture, including cattle ranches, apple orchards, wheat and soybean fields, and some five thousand acres of upland short-fiber cotton, which is making a slow but steady comeback.

This land was also valuable to the Native Americans who lived along the shores of the region's largest river. Numbering over ten thousand when the first Europeans arrived, they called themselves *yeh is-WAH h'reh* or *People of the River*. The first settlers named both the people and the river the Catawba. The Catawba hunted, fished, and planted corn along the Catawba River. The river was also their highway, and then, as now, the broad, swift waters flowed from the North Carolina mountains over two hundred miles south to Lake Wateree and on to the sea.

ROUTE 18

From Chester, follow U.S. Highway 321 north 9 miles to South Carolina Highway 909, and then head east on Highway 909. Highway 909 makes several turns then T-intersects with South Carolina Highway 9. Continue east on Highway 9 to South Carolina Highway 223 and turn east. Continue east 7 miles on Highway 223 to the intersection with U.S. Highway 21 (Catawba River Road). Follow U.S. 21 north. To reach Landsford State Canal Park, turn right (east) on Landsford Road and follow the signs to the park. After visiting the park, return to U.S. 21 and head north to South Carolina Highway 5. Follow Highway 5 east to U.S. Highway 521. Follow U.S. 521 north for a half mile to the entrance of Andrew Jackson State Park.

Celebrated author and farmer Dori Sanders picks peaches and tends her family's small roadside peach stand located on a quiet country road between the villages of Filbert and Clover.

Sunrise silhouettes a windmill and casts a golden glow across mist-laden meadows near Brattonsville.

An ancient cultivator stands guard in a dew-laden green meadow at Kings Mountain State Park.

Canals were a common means of moving goods before the railroad. The remains of the Lansford Canal and the reconstructed canal keeper's log house can be seen at Lansford Canal State Park.

In the mid-1800s, as more and more acreage in this area was dedicated to cotton, South Carolina's rivers became vital transportation routes that allowed the harvested cotton to reach the coast. The Catawba offered the promise of a cheap route to the coast and international markets, but the river was blocked by a series of rock-strewn rapids that were deadly to the heavy, cotton-laden barges. The solution was to build a canal that would bypass the rapids and gently lower the barges through a series of locks. At one time, more than a dozen of these canals existed in South Carolina.

Now the only remnant of South Carolina's canal era is preserved at Landsford Canal State Park, located about thirty miles southeast of Rock Hill off U.S. 321. The park features a log replica of the lockkeeper's home and a mile-and-a-half walking trail that follows the old tow path beside the ruins of the original canal to the locks and an old mill site. For nature lovers, the park offers stunning views of the wonderfully unspoiled Catawba River. The river's waters are exceptionally clean and pure, and every spring the shallows burst forth with the abundant blooms of one of the world's largest populations of rare and delicate Rocky Shoals Spider Lilies. Throughout the month, naturalist-led canoeing and hiking tours bring curious explorers to see the profusion of blooms, which reaches its peak in mid-May.

Farther north along the Catawba River, the Catawba tribe has made a promising comeback. In the heyday of the Landsford Canal, their tribe had dwindled through disease, war, and attrition to just 110 members. Today, they number almost two thousand, and the tribe is enthusiastically reclaiming its rich culture. Known as artists and craftsmen, the Catawba create pottery that has gained the notice of international collectors.

South Carolina Highway 5 passes through the Catawba's small reservation just outside Rock Hill. There, on the banks of the river, you will find the Catawba Cultural Preservation Project (off Reservation Road and Indian Trail). The building features a shop that offers Catawba pottery and other crafts. It also houses displays that relate the history of the tribe, which scholars say has lived in the Carolinas for more than forty-five hundred years.

About fifteen miles southeast of Rock Hill lies a state park named after one of South Carolina's most famous and accomplished native sons, Andrew Jackson. Jackson was born on a small farm near here and spent his boyhood in the region.

The only people who seem to have discovered this oasis of forests, lakes, and streams are local family campers and fishermen who come to try their luck with the bass and catfish that dwell in the park's lake. For a nominal fee, the park rangers will rent you a rowboat, so you can join them if you have fishing gear and a license. If you are feeling energetic, you can test your sneakers on one of the two trails that lead through the pretty forests of oak and cedar, or you can simply open up a lawn chair at the lake's edge and spend a few hours listening to the birds and watching the sunlight dancing across the water.

Born in a log farmhouse at the edge of the North Carolina–South Carolina frontier border in 1767, Andrew Jackson barely had a chance to grow up before his life was swept up in the turbulence of a new country. After he enlisted in the Continental Army at age thirteen to run messages as a courier, he was caught and imprisoned by the British. One story has it that when he refused to polish the boots of a British officer, the man slashed him with a sword, leaving Jackson with a badly injured hand and a deep hatred of the British.

Both Jackson and his brother, Robert, who was captured with him, contracted smallpox during their confinement, and his brother died just a few days after their release. Within a few years, virtually all of Jackson's immediate relatives were dead, a situation he attributed to the hardships brought on by the war.

When he was in his late teens, Jackson taught himself law and then moved to the western part of North Carolina and a year later to Tennessee to be a lawyer in the rough-and-tumble world of frontier justice. He was a proud firebrand, and as a young man, he fought and won a duel over a perceived insult to his wife.

While serving as a major general in the War of 1812, Jackson was given command of Tennessee troops against the Creek Indians. His resounding defeat of the Creeks in 1814 led to his command of American troops at the Battle of New Orleans, where he won a stunning surprise victory over vastly superior British forces. Considered stern but fair, Jackson was liked and respected by both his troops and officers, one of whom exclaimed that he was "as tough as an old hickory stick."

The nickname "Old Hickory" stuck, and as the hero of the New Orleans battle, he was easily elected to the U.S. Senate in 1823. Just a year later, he was running for president. He lost by a narrow margin, but won handily in 1828. As the first "frontier president," he championed the rights and freedoms of the common man and loathed leaders and politicians who emulated the European aristocracy. As president, Jackson brought sweeping reforms to the government and was easily re-elected in 1832. After two terms in office, he returned to his beloved Hermitage estate in Tennessee, where he remained active in public life until his death in 1845.

Known as "Old Hickory" for his toughness, Andrew Jackson was the hero of the Battle of New Orleans and the seventh president of the United States. Considered the first commoner president, he was proud of the fact that he was born in a log cabin near Waxhaw in South Carolina. Library of Congress

PART VII

THE UP COUNTRY

FACING PAGE:
An old water wheel stands along a cascading stream in the mountains near the Chattooga River. The largest waterwheel in the state, it once generated electricity for a nearby girls' school.

ABOVE:
The first colors of fall decorate a small tree standing near the misty cascade of Twin Falls.

In the western part of South Carolina, the land rises gently at first in the foothills and then dramatically ascends as you encounter the Appalachian escarpment. An ancient mountain chain, the Blue Ridge is named for the pallet of cool hues created by its mist-filled valleys. Through the years, the mountains have been a haven for those who knew them well and an impenetrable landscape for those who didn't. During the Revolutionary War, the British wisely never attempted to pursue Patriot troops into these rugged hills, and it was from here that the "Overmountain Men" from North Carolina and Tennessee poured in to help defeat the British at the Battle of Kings Mountain.

Perhaps no single road offers a more scenic and historically fascinating look at South Carolina than the 115-mile-long stretch of South Carolina State Highway 11, known as the Cherokee Foothills National Scenic Highway. True to its name, this route curves along the base of the mountains, following what was once a well-worn footpath used by the Cherokee natives long before the Revolutionary War. Starting along the shores of Lake Hartwell, this scenic highway traverses the western end of South Carolina's fertile piedmont, passing lakes and farmlands before rising into the rolling foothills, which are cut by sparkling streams that tumble out of the mountains.

The highway continues along the base of the steeply rising Appalachians in a long scimitar-like curve, offering occasional dramatic views across the hills and lush valleys checkered with small farms. Finally, the highway turns away from the mountains, crossing the plateau-like region around Gaffney, where peach orchards quilt the landscape and a great battle once determined the course of a young America.

Along the way a dozen or more side roads lead upward into the mountains, passing sparkling streams and apple orchards that thrive in the cooler elevations. They lead to streamside mills whose waterwheels turn in lazy cadence with the passing water and to timeless small settlements like Long Creek, where the homemade music of the mountains rings out of the country store every Saturday night.

MOUNTAIN TOWNS AND RAGING RIVERS
LAKE HARTWELL TO THE CHATTOOGA RIVER

ROUTE 19

Follow South Carolina Highway 11 (Cherokee Foothills National Scenic Highway) north from Interstate 85 to the junction with South Carolina State Highway 24 and turn north to Westminster. Follow U.S. Highway 76 northwest to the Chattooga River at the Georgia border.

The Cherokee Foothills National Scenic Highway begins at Exit 1 off Interstate 85 near the Georgia border. Here, serene Lake Hartwell is the northernmost of a chain of manmade lakes that form the heart of the Savannah River watershed. Created by a dam built in 1961, this large lake boasts over 968 miles of shoreline and is renowned to fishermen. The cool, deep waters—fed by the Tugaloo River and Lakes Jocassee and Keowee higher in the foothills—have created an ideal habitat for striped and largemouth bass, crappie, bream, and catfish of legendary size.

On summer mornings and late afternoons, the surface of the lake churns as fishing boats of every size and shape, ranging from simple flat-bottom

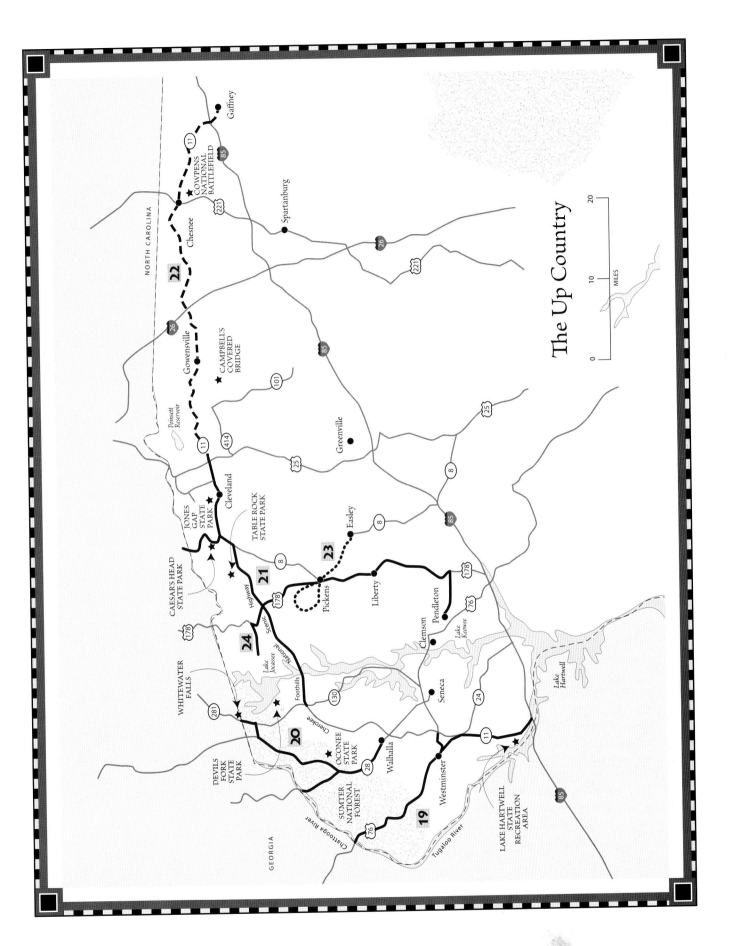

The Up Country

20
10
0
MILES

NORTH CAROLINA

Gaffney
11
COWPENS NATIONAL BATTLEFIELD
85
221
Chesnee
Spartanburg
26
221
22
26
Gowensville
CAMPBELL'S COVERED BRIDGE
101
Poinsett Reservoir
85
11
414
25
25
Greenville
8
Cleveland
JONES GAP STATE PARK
TABLE ROCK STATE PARK
8
23
Easley
85
CAESAR'S HEAD STATE PARK
21
178
Highway
Scenic
178
Pickens
Liberty
178
Pendleton
76
178
WHITEWATER FALLS
24
National
Lake Jocassee
Foothills
Clemson
Lake Keowee
281
130
Cherokee
Seneca
Lake Hartwell
DEVILS FORK STATE PARK
20
OCONEE STATE PARK
28
Walhalla
24
11
GEORGIA
Chattooga River
SUMTER NATIONAL FOREST
Westminster
19
76
Tugaloo River
LAKE HARTWELL STATE RECREATION AREA
85

Wild mountain laurel blooms in the woods of the Blue Ridge Mountains.

A rural shop near Long Creek offers one-stop shopping.

The lower end of Issaqueena Falls creates a misty veil as it tumbles into a clear mountain pool.

john boats to supercharged bass boats, take fishermen to their favorite fishing grounds. Houseboats are popular too, and they can often be seen anchored in quiet coves, where they float surrounded by the sights and sounds of nature.

One of the best places to enjoy the beauty of Lake Hartwell is at Lake Hartwell State Park. The park offers shady picnic sites along the lake, as well as RV and wilderness camping for those who want to stay longer. Most importantly, there are places to just sit and enjoy the ever-changing views of the lake.

The Cherokee Foothills Scenic Highway is dotted with crossroads that lead from the lowlands into the mountains. One of the most arresting of these is U.S. Highway 76, which starts in Westminster and leads to the raging waters of the wild and scenic Chattooga River. Westminster was—and, amazingly still is—a mill town, one of many towns in western South Carolina started or developed by the textile industry that was a once such a dominant economic force in the state. Today, many of those companies are gone, but in Westminster, Beacon Manufacturing still employs over 600 people. On "Mill Hill", you can still see the original mill houses that were once provided to workers by the company.

U.S. 76 continues into the heart of the mountains, climbing gently for several miles, then dropping suddenly as it races downhill into the narrow but verdant valley carved by the Chattooga River.

In the 1970s, as many of the rivers in South Carolina were being dammed for hydroelectric energy, local conservationists began a powerful movement to protect the remarkable beauty of this river. In 1972, Congress designated it the Chattooga National Wild and Scenic River, which effectively banned development. The Chattooga's popularity got a big boost that same year when it had a starring role in the hit movie *Deliverance* about a group of urban buddies who get in over their head while challenging its raging torrents.

As U.S. 76 crosses the river, you'll see an old iron bridge that seems as frail as the landscape is rugged, but don't cross the bridge yet. Instead pull into the parking lot just before the bridge and prepare to explore on foot. You can walk out on the bridge and gaze in both directions, but an even better idea is to follow the riverside trail upstream for a quarter mile to Bull Sluice Falls. This short rapid is one of the most challenging on the river. In the spring, it becomes a genuine Class V rapid that challenges even the best paddlers.

PARADISE AND THE PATH OF FAILED DREAMS
WALHALLA TO WHITEWATER FALLS

In 1849, an industrious group of German businessmen were looking for a suitable parcel on which they could create a new settlement in South Carolina. Their plan was simple: they would buy a large fertile expanse of land, subdivide it, and resell it to immigrants who they would recruit from Germany. After much deliberation, they chose a 17,000-acre tract of land near the base of the Appalachians. The town they laid out was named Walhalla, which is

ROUTE 20

From Walhalla take South Carolina Highway 28 northwest 6 miles to Stumphouse Tunnel Park. Continue north on Highway 28 to Russell Farmstead (on the left, just before the Georgia border). After visiting the farm, return south on Highway 28 to South Carolina Highway 107, where you'll turn north and follow Highway 107 to Walhalla Fish Hatchery. To reach Whitewater Falls, continue on Highway 107 until it intersects with S-37-413 (Wiggington Road), where you'll turn right. Follow S-37-413 until it reaches South Carolina Highway 130, where you'll turn left and drive to the Whitewater Falls parking area, about one mile across the North Carolina border.

German for paradise, and within two years, the first settlers arrived and began to clear and farm the land.

Just three years later, by coincidence, the South Carolina legislature was exploring how to develop a railway route that would link the port of Charleston to the booming frontier populations in the Ohio River Valley, in particular Knoxville, Tennessee. In order to reach the Midwest, however, the railroad would have to cross the formidable Blue Ridge Mountains. The first leg of the route required the construction of three tunnels that would have to be drilled through the hard granite mountains. The longest of these, Stumphouse Tunnel, would be over a mile long and require the labor of hundreds of workers. It would be constructed just six miles outside of Walhalla.

The classic rustic stone buildings of Paris Mountain State Park were built by the Civilian Conservation Corps in the 1930s. The CCC built many of the forty-six state parks that are located throughout South Carolina. Library of Congress

The fledgling community was excited at the prospect of a railway, which would bring with it the promise of employment and prosperity. But the first railway company contracted to build Stumphouse Tunnel was fired for incompetence after just a short time. A second company diligently started work on the mammoth project. A shanty town called Tunnel Hill soon went up to house the more than six hundred mostly Irish workers who labored on the tunnel. Yet the digging of the tunnel proceeded at the agonizingly slow pace of one hundred feet per month. Eventually, the second company abandoned the project after realizing how difficult it was.

By 1858, yet a third company had been contracted and had completed about two thirds of the tunnel and most of the grade through the mountains. But with the specter of the Civil War on the horizon, the South Carolina legislature decided the project was simply too costly and abandoned it. Today, all that remains of the tens of thousands of man-hours is the damp, cool entrance to Stumphouse Tunnel and the headstones of the graveyard that was created for those who died striving to build a dream.

Walhalla, however, very much exists, and every fall it celebrates its German heritage with a small but enthusiastic Oktoberfest. For those who arrive at any other time of the year, Walhalla is a classic example of small-town America, with a variety of interesting shops housed in well-maintained historic buildings.

Leaving Wallhalla, Highway 28 quickly begins to rise into the mountains. You'll eventually see the entrance to Stumphouse Mountain Park on the right. The park road leads to the legendary unfinished railway tunnel, but first turn off to visit Issaqueena Falls. One of the most resplendent of all South Carolina waterfalls, Issaqueena is a misty cascade that tumbles 100 feet down the green-forested cliffs.

The granite face of Table Rock Mountain is reflected in the waters of a small lake in Table Rock State Park.

A mountain trail leads to an overlook a thousand feet above the waters of Lake Jocassee.

The spectacular view from Caesar's Head overlook takes in the dramatic rise of the Appalachian escarpment and the foothills of western South Carolina.

According to legends, the falls were named for a Cherokee woman who married an Englishman in the 1700s. She was subsequently recaptured by Cherokees and, while prisoner, overheard their plans for attacking nearby settlements. She managed to escape, and with Cherokee warriors in hot pursuit, she faked jumping off the precipice of the falls, grabbing a branch as she fell and hiding behind the falls under a rock overhang. She later made it to an English fort in time to warn settlers of the pending attack.

If you return toward Walhalla on Highway 28 and take the turnoff onto Highway 107 North, you will find two great places with hiking trails in this area. The first is Oconee State Park, a pretty 1,165-acre park with trails that follow rushing mountain streams and lead to secluded lakes. The second is Cherry Hill Recreation Area. The trails here range from the easy half-mile Cherry Hill Nature Trail to the more challenging Winding Stairs Trail and the Big Bend Trail that leads to the Chattooga River just 2.7 miles away.

Beyond Cherry Hill Recreation Area, Highway 107 curves even more as it ranges deeper into the mountains. If you watch closely on the left, you'll see a turnoff to the Walhalla Fish Hatchery. A creation of Franklin D. Roosevelt's Civilian Conservation Corps (CCC) in the 1930s, this facility now annually raises over 500,000 rainbow, brown, and brook trout for release in the surrounding mountain streams.

A couple of miles past the fish hatchery on Highway 107 is a right turn onto S-37-413 (Wiggington Road), which leads to a well-marked overlook. This spot offers a stunning vista of Lake Jocassee, nestled in the rolling hills over a thousand feet below. Farther along S-37-413, turn left onto South Carolina Highway 130, and just over the border into North Carolina, a parking area marks the start of a short walk to Upper Whitewater Falls. The first of two cascades, the falls drop more than four hundred feet as the river descends into South Carolina, dropping another four hundred feet at Lower Whitewater Fall before tumbling into Lake Jocassee's deep cerulean waters.

INTO THE GREAT BLUE HILLS OF GOD
SALEM TO U.S. HIGHWAY 25

As the Cherokee Foothills National Scenic Highway (Highway 11) passes Salem, it draws closer to the dramatically beautiful Appalachian escarpment that rises more than two thousand feet above the surrounding foothills. These were the mountains that the Cherokee called *Sah-Ka-Na-Ga*, meaning *great blue hills of God*. English tongues corrupted *Sah-Ka-Na-Ga* to "Seneca," which also became the name of a prominent local Cherokee town. That town disappeared after the forced expulsion of the Cherokee in 1838, but an English town built around a railroad station southeast of Walhalla borrowed the name, and it stuck.

As Highway 11 continues north and east from Salem, the surrounding foothills become more prominent and the road passes several tumbling

ROUTE 21

Follow South Carolina Highway 11 (Cherokee Foothills National Scenic Highway) east from Salem about 35 miles to the junction with U.S. Highway 25. For the side trip to Caesar's Head and Pretty Place, follow U.S. Highway 276 north from Highway 11 to Caesar's Head State Park. Continue north on U.S. 276 to reach S-23-15 (Solomon Jones Road), where you will turn right and follow the signs to Camp Greenville (YMCA) and Symmes Chapel (Pretty Place).

mountain streams. In the 1700s, these streams guided trappers and traders into the mountains. A century later, they powered simple grist and cotton mills. But it wasn't until the twentieth century that their latent energy was fully harnessed by technology.

In 1935, less than 2 percent of the state's 168,000 farms had electricity. That year, South Carolina began an aggressive and far-reaching plan to build dams for hydroelectric power. The first dams spanned the Cooper and Santee rivers southeast of Columbia. They were followed by dams on the Wateree and the Congaree, and a complex series of dams along the Savannah, which not only provided power but also controlled the flooding that cyclically ravaged the Low Country.

The last dams constructed in South Carolina were those here in the rolling Appalachian foothills of the state's far western corner. The Keowee Dam was built in 1967, and the Jocassee Dam followed in 1973. These dams provide the state with more electricity than it needs, allowing it to sell power to surrounding states. The Jocassee Dam also created one of the loveliest mountain lakes on the eastern seaboard. Nestled among thousand-foot-high rounded peaks, Lake Jocassee's sapphire waters are brimming with trout and bass and have become a magnet for sports fishermen. The beauty of the area has also attracted developers, who have created extensive communities of upscale lakefront and mountainside homes with prices as breathtaking as the views.

If you don't happen to have a small fortune to plunk down for one of these elegant homes, you can still get a good view of Lake Jocassee at Devils Fork State Park. This quiet and pretty park is popular with family campers and fishermen. In summer, wildflowers bloom in the meadows and views encompass the lake's sparkling waters and lead beyond and upward into the misty mountains.

Highway 11 crosses the northern end of Lake Keowee just below Lake Jocassee. On the east side of Lake Keowee is Keowee-Toxaway State Park. The one hundred–acre park is another place to stretch your legs and enjoy the beauty of the lake and surrounding mountains. A small museum here tells the absorbing but ultimately tragic story of the Cherokee Indians who once called these mountains home. The park also offers a couple of hiking trails, including the moderately strenuous but highly rewarding four-mile long Raven Rock Trail. It leads up McKinney Mountain to Raven Rock, giving adventurers panoramic views of the foothills and surrounding mountains.

Serious hikers will also appreciate Table Rock State Park. This 3,000-acre park lies a few miles northwest of Lake Keowee at the very base of the mountains. The park is named for the mountaintop's sheer granite cliffs, which are visible for miles around. It is here, atop this rocky fortress, that the Cherokee believed the gods dined. As Highway 11 passes through the park, it offers everchanging views of the park's lakes and meadows and the sheer granite face of Table Rock Mountain two-thousand-feet above.

An early morning autumn frost decorates this barn and meadow near Caesar's Head State Park. With elevations reaching three thousand feet, the Blue Ridge Mountains offer the coolest climate in South Carolina.

The small chapel at Pretty Place offers one of the most stunning sunrises in the state.

The park's nearly eight-mile round-trip Pinnacle Trail is a popular but strenuous hike. It leads to lovely Mill Creek Falls and then on to the spectacular mountain views from Bald Rock and the 3,452-foot-high summit of Pinnacle Mountain. The park also offers plenty of shorter but equally rewarding trails, and it boasts two lakes that are popular with fishermen. For those wanting to extend their stay, there is a large campground.

Two miles east of the entrance to Table Rock State Park, watch for Aunt Sue's Country Corner (it will be on the left). This small group of shops, housed in log cabins, offers an intriguing array of artwork and crafts created by local artisans. On summer and fall weekends, this can be a lively place; a musician plays on the porch, and tour buses drop off throngs who crowd the bustling restaurant and ice cream parlor. This is the best restaurant in this area and worth the wait even on busy days. You can put your name on the list and then wander the shops until they call you—literally by shouting your name down the row of porches.

The countryside beyond Aunt Sue's is full of gently rolling forested hills and small country farms, meadows, and orchards. Many of the side roads are fun to explore, and one of the most interesting is U.S. Highway 276. Heading north, it leads steeply upward to magnificent Caesar's Head State Park and the lovely Symmes Chapel at Pretty Place.

Perched at an elevation of 3,266 feet, Caesar's Head offers one of the state's most spectacular views, encompassing the dramatic rise of the Appalachian escarpment, the lovely rolling foothills, and the distant farmlands of the piedmont to the southeast. Visitors to Caesar's Head State Park must walk a hundred yards to the viewing area, which sits on the sheer edge of the rock formation that gives the park its name. To one side of the look-off, a stairway leads down about thirty feet to a cleft in the rock and a second viewing point.

Along with Jones Gap State Park and other public lands, the 7,500-acre Caesar's Head State Park is part of the vast Mountain Bridge Wilderness Area, which features more than fifty miles of excellent hiking trails.

U.S. 276 follows the ridge of the mountain for several miles, eventually crossing into North Carolina. Right at the state line, watch on the right for S-23-15, or Solomon Jones Road, and then follow the signs to the Greenville YMCA camp. This road is lovely and leads right through the heart of the camp, which was built in 1912. (Do watch your speed, as there are many children about, especially in summer.) At the end of the road lies tiny Symmes Chapel, built in 1941 and maintained now as part of the YMCA camp.

After parking in the nearby lot, step inside this unique house of worship, and you will immediately know why it is known as "Pretty Place." This lovely chapel without walls sits at the very edge of the escarpment some two thousand feet above the valleys below. The view faces east, making Pretty Place the perfect place to observe a sunrise. If you come that early, you may have the place entirely to yourself, or you may be joined by small, quiet groups of young people from the camp. Unlike Caesar's Head, there are seldom crowds here.

The pillars of the chapel have small memorial plaques featuring quotes on nature and spirituality that are taken from the Bible and the works of popular writers such as Kahlil Gibran. Sunday mornings are reserved for services, and all are welcome. Weddings happen here often in summer, so it helps to call ahead to see if the chapel will be open to the public.

If you want to experience the sunrise, be sure to arrive a half hour before the publicized sunrise, as from this elevation, you are looking down on the horizon and the sun will appear earlier. It is virtually impossible to stand at this spot, watching the first rays of sun light the ancient mountains and fill the misty valleys with a rosy glow, and not be moved deeply, whatever your beliefs. Later, as the sun warms the mountainsides, you may be treated to the sight of a hawk as it soars along the mountain flanks, riding the rising thermals in a timeless dance of life.

Upon returning back to Highway 11 and heading five miles east, you'll find that one of the area's most popular waterfalls, Wildcat Branch, tumbles right to the edge of the road. The falls are only visible for a moment from the road, so watch closely for a parking area on the left. In summer, local vendors sometimes offer crafts, jam, and locally harvested honey from their vehicles in the parking area. The falls are small but lovely, dropping about forty feet in two cascades.

The highway continues through the pastoral mountain landscape to U.S. Highway 25, which leads to Poinsett Bridge and the unheralded beauty of Jones Gap State Park.

MORGAN'S TRIUMPH
U.S. HIGHWAY 25 TO GAFFNEY

The final section of the Cherokee Foothills Scenic Highway gradually moves away from the mountains and into the fertile orchard lands of the state's northwestern corner. The road travels through a varied scenic landscape of hills and farms, passing the turnoff for Campbell's Bridge, the last covered bridge in South Carolina, near Gowensville. Many miles further on, your gentle re-entry to civilization comes in the form of the pretty little town of Chesnee.

There are two things you must do in Chesnee. One is to visit the Carolina Foothills Artisans Center. Modeled after the famous Blue Ridge Folk Art Center near Ashville, North Carolina, and housed in a beautifully restored commercial building downtown, the 2,000-square-foot gallery presents the work of more than 100 regional artists and craftspeople. The attractive space is filled with pottery, folk art, woodwork, paintings, and fine-art photography. It is a great place to wile away an hour just browsing.

The other thing you must do in Chesnee is to stop for lunch at Bantam Chef, the excellent and charming 1950s-style restaurant that's filled to the brim with the owner's unique collection of memorabilia, including a full-size Studebaker. This is not the time to worry about your diet, though. Toss it overboard and relive the good old days with a big, juicy hamburger, french fries, and a thick and frosty milkshake. Life doesn't get much better!

ROUTE 22

Follow South Carolina Highway 11 (Cherokee Foothills National Scenic Highway) from the junction with U.S. Highway 25 east about 62 miles to Gaffney.

Historic re-enactors portraying Loyalist soldiers fire their muskets in unison during a mock battle at Walnut Grove Plantation.

During a weekend of Revolutionary War re-enactments at Walnut Grove Plantation, a history buff portrays a colonial-era Cherokee Indian.

This simple monument at Cowpens National Battlefield honors a battle that many historians believe turned the tide of the Revolutionary War.

The Peachoid water tower in Gaffney makes an unmistakable declaration that this is peach country. Rising high above the surrounding countryside, the peach holds a million gallons of water, and the leaf is sixty feet long and weighs seven tons.

The drive east of Chesnee on Highway 11 leads two hundred years back in time. Although most Americans are familiar with the Revolutionary War battles of Bunker Hill and Valley Forge, few know that the most decisive battles of the war against the British were fought in the woods and fields of this quiet corner of South Carolina. If you blink, you might miss the entrance to Cowpens National Battlefield (about two miles east of Chesnee), where one of the most dramatic stories of young America played out.

The year was 1781, and the struggle for independence had reached a crucial tipping point. So far, the war had progressed poorly for the colonial forces. Routs and defeats had demoralized their armies, and desertions were commonplace. The British, on the other hand, were becoming bolder, convinced that their victory was imminent. They had arrived by sea to subdue the southern colonies in 1778. The quick fall of Savannah was followed by easy victories at Charleston and inland at Camden. Then, in the winter of 1780, came the stunning defeat of a thousand British troops by a rugged, undisciplined force of "Overmountain Men" at Kings Mountain.

The following January, the Americans needed to prove that their victory at Kings Mountain wasn't a lucky accident, and the British were determined to demonstrate their military superiority. In a daring move, a newly assigned Patriot general, Nathaniel Greene, split his forces, sending General Daniel Morgan with five hundred battle-hardened colonials and one thousand poorly-trained militia inland toward the mountains. This forced General Charles Cornwallis to split his forces. He sent his favorite officer, "Bloody" Banastre Tarleton, and twelve hundred British regular forces in hot pursuit of Morgan.

With Tarleton on his heels, Morgan chose the relatively open ground of Hiram Saunder's cow pens to make a stand. Morgan's plan was simple. He told his relatively inexperienced militia troops to get off "just two good shots" and they could go home to their families. The militia would fire and fall back, enticing the overconfident British to chase after them into a hail of musket fire that would be delivered by Morgan's battle-tested Continental Army.

All went as planned—at first. However, at a critical moment in the battle, the experienced colonial forces mistook an order and marched to the rear, appearing as though they were retreating. As the British ran in chaos after them, Morgan drew his sword and rode to rally them. With the British almost at their backs, the mass of Continental soldiers turned as one and fired a devastating volley into the British ranks, then charged, scattering the British in panic.

Within minutes, the tide of the battle turned and Tarleton was forced to flee with less than a tenth of his original force, leaving behind 110 dead and more than 800 captured. General Greene pressed his advantage, pursuing Cornwallis to the north and east. After another year of fighting with no clear victories, Cornwallis withdrew to Yorktown, where he was trapped by General Washington's army and forced to surrender.

The Cherokee Foothills Scenic Highway (Highway 11) passes by this historically important and now tranquil battleground and ends in Gaffney at the junction with Interstate 85. This is peach country, and near this intersection stands what is certainly the most photographed water tower in the state: Gaffney's famous "Peachoid." This gigantic, brilliantly painted, peach-shaped tower rises above the landscape, creating a clever advertisement and a point of pride for residents.

The tower's impressiveness is reflected in its dimensions. Built in 1981 by the Chicago Bridge and Iron Company, the foundation required ten million pounds of concrete. The forming of the steel sections took over five months, and they were assembled with over a mile and a half of welds. The peach's deep cleft was formed with false iron panels that were added to the tank. The Peachoid's stem is twelve feet long and a foot and a half in diameter. Its sixty-foot-long leaf weighs over seven tons.

The final paint job on the tower was rendered by an artist who specialized in gigantic representations, and it required more than fifty gallons of special custom-mixed paint to represent the colors of locally grown peaches.

But Gaffney's love affair with peaches doesn't stop with the Peachoid. If you happen to be here in July, the town holds the largest peach festival in the state, with a fair, live music, and entertainment for the whole family—not to mention, of course, lots of ripe, juicy peaches.

MILLS AND MOUNTAINS
EASLEY TO GOLDEN CREEK, HAGOOD, AND MEECE MILLS

Around 1815, William O'Dell began to construct a grist mill on the banks of the lovely, tumbling Golden Creek. O'Dell built a solid dam across the stream to create the reservoir that would keep his mill running even through dry spells and channeled the reservoir's water down to his mill. As a seemingly inexhaustible stream of immigrants arrived in South Carolina, the number of farms in the western part of the state was burgeoning, and those farms required mills to grind their corn and wheat crops and to gin cotton.

Today, these country roads look little changed from the ones farmers followed more than a hundred years ago as they guided their loaded wagons from the outskirts of Easley past pretty little Enon Church to the shady glen where O'Dell built his mill. By 1835, O'Dell's business had grown to the point that he could add a cotton press and cotton gin to the site. The mill remained in operation for over a century, but by 1940 the big industrial mills in Easley and other Up Country towns made the aging Golden Creek Mill obsolete, and it fell into disrepair and crumbled.

In 1985, a retired minister, Leroy Stewart, bought the property where the old Golden Mill once stood. Mills were a passion for Stewart—he had dreamed of one day owning and operating a water-powered mill. As he searched the country for a restorable mill, he collected bits and pieces of

ROUTE 23

Take South Carolina Highway 8 northwest from Easley. Roughly 2 miles past the intersection with South Carolina Highway 93, turn left on Brazeale Road and continue 1/2 mile to Enon Church Road. Turn left on Enon Church Road and continue for 1 1/2 miles. Look closely on the right for parking for Golden Creek Mill. After returning to Highway 8, turn left (north) to Pickens. Once downtown, turn left (west) on South Carolina Highway 183 and then make a quick right heading north on U.S. Highway 178. Continue north on U.S. 178 for 3 miles until you see Hagood Road on your left. Follow it northward to Hagood Mill. To reach Yoder's at Meese Mill, continue north on Hagood Road to Preston McDaniel Road, where you'll go left (west) 1 1/2 miles until you can turn left on Meese Mill Road. Continue south on Meese Mill Road until you can turn left (east) onto Reese Mill Road. To complete the route, follow Reese Mill Road east until it intersects with U.S. 178 in Pickens.

The waters of Golden Creek have been used to grind corn for almost two hundred years. The first Golden Creek Mill was constructed here around 1815.

A boy examines an antique farm truck loaded with chickens, parked beside a log cabin at the Hagood Mill Historic Site.

Lovely, tranquil Breazeale Road travels through the fertile red farmlands of South Carolina's western foothills. The road is named for one of the first families to settle in the region.

mill works and machinery. When he could find no standing mills, he came back to his native South Carolina and decided to rebuild the mill that had once stood along Golden Creek.

He relocated the mill to a more advantageous spot on the other side of the stream and began to build. The labor of love took him seven years. It finally opened to the public in 1992.

Today, Stewart operates the mill every third Saturday of the month and on a flexible schedule other times. During the school year, a seemingly endless stream of student groups visit the site to see how the generations before them milled grains. Visitors are welcome at the mill site on any day. If Stewart is there, he will usually open the mill so you can tour it and buy a bag of mill-ground cornmeal. There is a small picnic area a few paces from the mill, and on days when the mill is operating, you can enjoy a simple meal by the stream, watching the wheel turn and listening to the burble of the water rushing past.

After visiting Golden Creek Mill, return on Highway 8 to the outskirts of Easley before turning left to Pickens. Named for Revolutionary War hero Andrew Pickens, the town was originally settled fourteen miles to the west of its current location. It was moved in 1868, after the original Pickens District was split into present-day Pickens and Oconee counties. Because of the split, the original town of Pickens, the county seat, was no longer located in Pickens County. In those days, buildings were valuable and labor was cheap, so dismantling the town and moving it fourteen miles east to reassemble it in the redrawn county seemed like a good idea.

Among the buildings that were moved was the elegant Greek Revival home of Judge James Hagood. It is still standing and is now known as the Hagood-Maudlin House. The house has been carefully restored and contains an interesting collection of historic furniture and silver. It also houses the Irma Morris Museum of Fine Arts. The house is only open Saturday afternoons or by appointment.

In addition to being a judge, Hagood was an entrepreneur. He built and operated a mill on land that belonged to his wealthy father, Benjamin Hagood. Known as Hagood Mill, it not only served a commercial purpose, but was also a social hub in this small settlement. Here, farmers would share the news of the day and swap stories, while children would play in the stream as their father's corn was being ground.

Inside, the corn was fed into a chute that channeled it into the hub of the top mill wheel. As the corn was forced between the spinning top wheel and the stationary bottom wheel, it was cut finer and finer by the sharp edges cut into the granite face of both wheels. As the ground corn reached the outside of the wheels, it dropped into a hopper, and the machinery gently shook it along sifting screens, separating it into fine flour, semicoarse meal, grits, and then the coarsest feed. Throughout the grinding process, farmers kept a close eye on the millwright, who was allowed one full scoop of meal—only one—for every twelve and a half pounds of corn that was ground.

The Hagood Mill still stands on its original site just north of Pickens. The fully operational mill was made a national historic site in 1972. Since then, several other historic buildings have been moved to the site, including a restored moonshine still, a blacksmith shop, and the 1791 Murphee-Hookingsworth Cabin, a superb example of a traditional Up Country hewn-log cabin.

Like the Golden Creek Mill, the Hagood Mill is an overshot mill, which means the water strikes the wheel at the top and the weight of it moves the wheel downwards. These were far more efficient than the older undershot wheels that were turned by the force of a swift flow of water passing underneath the wheel. The Hagood Mill developed twenty-two horsepower and was unusual in that the dam that created its reservoir is located over a quarter mile away, at the top of the hill behind the mill. An earthen ditch or millrace channels the water from the dam to the mill. Today, the mill operates only on the third Saturday of every month, but the property is open for touring daily.

The Hagood Mill fell into disrepair before a major renovation was undertaken in the 1970s. Today, it is one of the oldest grist mills in operation in South Carolina. Pendleton District Commission

The number of mills that once operated in this area is reflected in the names of the roads that lead through the steeply rolling and heavily forested hills. Meese Mill Road leads to Reese Mill Road, but before it does, it stops at Yoder's at Meese Mill, the last mill on this tour. The original mill on this site was probably another overshot mill similar to Hagood Mill (not surprising, considering it was also built by Hagood). Later, this mill was bought by Bob Meese and renamed Meese Mill. In the 1930s, it was rebuilt as a turbine mill, and it remained running until 1964. In more than a century of operation, Meece Mill ground both wheat and corn, and it operated as a hammer mill.

Today, Yoder's at Meese Mill serves just as practical a purpose—filling the hungry bellies of backroads wanderers. On the third Saturday of each month—from 11 a.m. to 4 p.m. and coinciding with the public hours of the Golden Creek and Hagood mills—the Mennonite Yoder family, along with a small army of their friends and helpers, serve a wonderful country barbeque-style lunch with home-baked desserts here. The meals are legendary, and it's best to arrive early to avoid the long lines at the door. Diners eat at tables scattered in the various rooms of the pleasantly decorated mill, and there are locally made crafts and country foods for sale throughout the building. An open porch at one end of the rambling building offers a pleasant view of the woods and the rushing stream, which once powered the mighty turbines that ground corn and wheat for a hungry nation.

Today Pendleton's historic Farmer's Hall has been beautifully renovated and houses a fine restaurant that is the focal point of the town square.

The historic buildings surrounding Pendleton's invitingly shady, green town square house a variety of gift, antique, and specialty shops as well as restaurants.

Built in 1797 on land donated by local printer John Miller, The Old Stone Church, near Pendleton, was the first church in South Carolina to admit slaves into the congregation. Among those buried in the cemetery are Revolutionary War General Robert Anderson and at least two men who died in duels.

True to its name, Twin Falls drops in two distinct cascades as Reedy Cove Creek splits before dropping in a frothy veil over a rocky escarpment in Eastatoe Valley.

ROUTE 24

Follow South Carolina Highway 88 east from Pendleton to Ashtabula Plantation. After visiting the plantation, return on Highway 88 to Pendleton. Once downtown, head east on Main Street, then bear right (heading south) on Lebanon Road. At the intersection with Breazeale Road, veer left and continue east until you reach the junction with U.S. Highway 178. At the crossroads, head north on U.S. 178. Three miles or so past the intersection with South Carolina Highway 11, turn left (heading west) on Cleo Chapman Road. Continue about 3 miles to Eastatoe Community Road and bear right. Follow Eastatoe Community Road for one mile, turning right on Falls Road. About a mile farther, start watching for signs to a parking area for Twin Falls.

For an alternate return, you can go back to Cleo Chapman Road and head west, following the road through the Eastatoe Valley, eventually turning south on Granny Gear or Roy Jones Road to return to Highway 11.

If there is a single community that embodies all the charms of small-town South Carolina, it would be Pendleton. The quaint downtown, with its shady and inviting town square, is surrounded by century-old commercial buildings with big glass windows and colorful awnings. Pendleton presents such a classic small-town America scene that you could easily imagine Andy Griffith, Opie, and Aunt Bea strolling along the sidewalk enjoying ice cream cones and chatting with friends passing by.

In recent years, the buildings have been pleasantly (but not overly) gentrified, making the town square an inviting place to roam and window shop. At one end of the green stands the elegant, pillared Farmer's Hall, built in 1828. At one time, farmer's society buildings like this stood in most small Carolina towns. Now this building houses one of the region's finest restaurants and is a great place for lunch or dinner. The restaurant's open-air patio with tables shaded by colorful umbrellas is a great place to sit, enjoy a meal, and watch the comings and goings in the pretty town square.

If you happen to be in town on a Sunday afternoon, head east on South Carolina Highway 88 for a mile or so and watch on your left for Ashtabula Plantation (open from 2 to 6 p.m. on Sundays in April through October). This elegant Greek Revival house hearkens back to the days prior to the Civil War, when cotton was king and wealthy plantations were strung like pearls along the banks of nearby Eighteen Mile Creek.

In many ways, the story of Ashtabula mirrors the history of South Carolina itself. If you walk around the main house, you come to a charming brick structure that stands behind it. This is the dwelling that Thomas Lofton built shortly after 1790, the year he was given a grant of 320 acres for his service as sheriff.

In 1820, the first frame house was built on the plantation, and as the size of Up Country plantations grew and fortunes increased, the home was expanded to its current size. Throughout this period, the original home served as a "dependency"—an all-purpose term for an outbuilding where the cooking and most of the daily work of the house was performed. Inside, the main house is furnished with period antiques, and outside the gardens and porch swing offer an open invitation to dawdle.

After returning to Pendleton on Highway 88, go east on Main Street until you can bear right on Lebanon Road. This road leads through a gently rolling countryside of small farms and woodlands, passing the perfectly whitewashed fences of horse country. There are working cattle ranches and well-tended pasturelands here as well. If you watch closely, you'll spot Breazeale Road; turn left on it. This short, postcard-worthy road is named after the Breazeale family, who moved into the area with the earliest settlers. Their original homestead sits amid fields close to the road, and the lovely farmland scenery here has probably changed little in the past hundred years.

After heading north on U.S. Highway 178, the similarly bucolic rural landscape eventually includes the tiny hamlet of Liberty and later Pickens. Beyond Pickens, the hills become true foothills, and the landscape becomes forested, now and then offering views of the Blue Ridge Mountains. When U.S. 178 crosses South Carolina Highway 11 (the Cherokee Foothills National Scenic Highway), it starts rising up the Blue Ridge Escarpment. Three miles or so past this intersection, watch for Cleo Chapman Road on your left.

Don't let the roughness of Bob's Place, the country biker bar that marks the corner, fool you. This tiny lane descends and winds through Eastatoe Valley, one of the prettiest hidden valleys in the state. Three miles in, you'll reach an intersection with Eastatoe Community Road, which leads to the right and winds between ever higher mountains into a blind valley carved by the sparkling Eastatoe Creek. (The creek can be seen here and there through the foliage.)

Your destination is a dirt parking lot off Falls Road, where you will stop and stroll along a lovely short path that wanders along the rocky, forested banks of the swiftly flowing Reedy Cove Creek. At the end of the trail, is an observation platform with a panoramic view of Twin Falls—two distinct cascades that form as the creek tumbles a hundred or more feet down the rocks and rushes off to join Eastatoe Creek.

This spot can be busy on summer weekends, but at any other time you may have it all to yourself. Here the air is alive with mountain breezes and the music of birdsong and the distant thunder of the cascading falls.

In the nineteenth and early twentieth centuries, most Southern towns had farmer's societies. This farmer's society meeting hall in Pendleton is a classic example of Greek Revival architecture. Pendleton District Commission

INDEX

About the Authors

Paul Franklin is a travel photographer and writer whose work has appeared in numerous national publications, including *Yankee, WoodenBoat, Travel America, Coast to Coast, Harrowsmith,* and others. He and Nancy Mikula recently collaborated on *South Carolina's Plantations and Historic Homes* for Voyageur Press. Paul also photographed Voyageur Press' *Our Washington, D.C.* Other books he wrote include *The Barnes and Noble Complete Guide to the Public Parks and Gardens of Washington, D.C.,* the Eyewitness Travel Guides *Canada* and *Southwest USA & Las Vegas,* and the *AAA Spiral Guide to Washington, D.C.* He is a member of the American Society of Media Photographers and the American Society of Travel Writers.

Author and researcher Nancy Mikula has a passion for exploring backroads and discovering little-known historic sites. Her articles on travel, historic, and human-interest subjects have appeared in numerous magazines in the United States and Canada, including *Maturity, Leisureways,* and *Writer's Digest.* Aside from collaborating on *South Carolina's Plantations and Historic Homes,* she recently authored the *Top Ten Guide to Santa Fe and Taos* and is co-author of several books, including the Eyewitness Travel Guide *Arizona & the Grand Canyon.* She spends her winters enjoying the warmth of coastal South Carolina.